SOBER SPRING

Addiction and Recovery

Robert F. Bollendorf

With additional articles on addiction and recovery by Rob
Bollendorf Ed.D. CADC , Rob Castillo LCSW,
ICAADC, MISA II, Kimberly
Groll LCPC, CADC, CAMT and Frank Salvatini
M.Ed. CSADC, NCAC II, MISA II

authorHOUSE®

AuthorHouse™
1663 Liberty Drive
Bloomington, IN 47403
www.authorhouse.com
Phone: 1 (800) 839-8640

Published by AuthorHouse   06/27/2016

ISBN: 978-1-5246-0987-0 (sc)
ISBN: 978-1-5246-0986-3 (e)

Library of Congress Control Number: 2016908218

Print information available on the last page.

SOBER SPRING

DEDICATION

IT SEEMS AT CRUCIAL BEGINNINGS of my life, there was a person named Fred there to help me along and show me the ropes. When I started my life, there was my father. When I started my career, there was Fred Holbeck, who became my mentor. Finally, when I became interested in the disease of alcoholism and how it affects the family, there was Fred Klein. This book is dedicated to them and to their families.

ACKNOWLEDGMENTS

IT SCARES ME THAT I may forget to mention one or more of the people who played a significant part in the writing of this book. To you I must apologize. If it's any consolation, I'll probably wake up one night and remember you and not get back to sleep because of the guilt I feel. It is also difficult to determine who contributed the most, so I've decided to name people in the order—to the best of my recollection—in which they entered my story, rather than by their relative importance. To start with, I'd like to note some of the people who were involved in the field of intervention and/or working with chemically-dependent families before me. My thanks to Vernon Johnson for developing an "intervention" in the first place. Thanks to Claudia Black and Sharon Wegscheider for their early work with dependent families.

On a more personal note, I guess I'd have to start with my sister, Maggie Klein. She was an early reader of this book, but, more importantly, when I was a graduate student impressed with my massive knowledge and convinced that the alcoholic was involved in a game, not a disease, she taught me otherwise. Next I'd have to mention John Daniels because it was he who taught me about interventions and also because he wasn't afraid to tell me that the book made him cry. Then there was Bill Makely and his wife Ethel. Without Bill's editing, I probably would have been too embarrassed to send this book to a publisher; but it was also Bill and Ethel who convinced me in the beginning that perhaps I could actually write a book.

The next person to be involved was Ann Gallagher.

She not only helped type, but was also very encouraging.

Early readers were Cathy Pammer, Maria Doherty, Priscilla Cross, Barb Marsh, Nancy Clough, Ruth Etheridge, and my daughter Becky who also did some typing. Those also helping with typing and encouragement included Bev Garrett and Vicki Willey.

I received technical advice from Ken Blauw, Dick Dobbs, Rita Bobrowski, Pam Hugelan, Don Krzyzak, Mary Lou Eickleman and Bill Vlasek; but they were also helpful because they're friends who believe in me. Along that same line, I'd like to add the students and clients who all contributed to the book with their life stories and support.

I decided for this second edition of the book to leave most of the original acknowledgements unchanged.

I've lost touch with some of those people, but they still contributed. I thank Joe Barillari for having the confidence in me and in the book to publish it again and to give me a chance to add some ideas to the new version.

CHAPTER **1**

· · · • • • • • • • • • ● • • • • • • • • • · ·

WINTER DIES SLOWLY IN NORTHERN Wisconsin and the coming of spring is more of a whisper than a pronouncement.

It's not so much the cold and snow that make people hunger for spring; it's the grey skies and streets and sidewalks.

It's the frozen lakes and rivers. It's the lifelessness of the trees and woods. Residents search the dirty snowbanks for a trickle of melting snow, or sniff the air for that scent they have come to know. Neither sign is an assurance that winter is over; it is just the hope of things to come.

On this Sunday morning, there was the first trickle of water from the banks and the scent was in the air. Molly Brandt was on her way to church. It was much too cold to have the window open, but she cracked it a little to let the spring fragrance into the car. A southern breeze had warmed the temperature all night so that it was warmer now than when she had gone to bed. Although it was just past dawn, she could tell already that it would be the first warm day.

Molly was a serious woman in her forties. She and her husband, Hank, had five children. They were all—perhaps with one exception—good kids. Molly could be attractive but she usually wore her hair in a plain bun and never fussed much with her clothes or makeup. She was the part-time music teacher at the grade school in town as well as the organist for the church. She was an excellent musician.

This morning she was a little more cheerful than usual
-perhaps because of the scent of spring in the air and because her friend Josh was out of the hospital. He had gone in for more surgery and although she had visited him there, it wasn't the same as seeing him around town.

Dr. Joshua Krueger was the one person in the world Molly could really talk to. He'd been the only doctor in town for as long as she could remember. Rushed as he usually was, he always seemed to find time for Molly and her problems.

They had been close ever since he helped her deal with the early death of both her parents in a car accident.

Now, married with five children of her own, Molly always seemed to be going to "Dr. Josh" for something. There were school checkups and shots and bouts with the flu. Her family also seemed to have more than its share of illness and accidents.

Once, a couple of years ago during an office visit, she had talked to him about arguing with her husband and he had asked what they fought about. She had told him "Alcohol, mostly."

At first he had tried to convince her that Hank worked hard and had the right to stop for a beer or two. But then he found out how much Hank drank and how long he stayed out. He became more compassionate and listened. He had been listening ever since. Once or twice he had suggested professional help. At other times he suggested Al-Anon, a program for people with a close relationship to an alcoholic.

This shocked Molly. She wasn't sure that Hank was an alcoholic and thought professional help was too drastic a step.

She continued to talk to Josh about it, however, since he was the only one she had who would listen when she needed to pour out her heart.

Josh was a quiet, even shy, man. He had never married. Rumors—and there were plenty—had it that the girl he loved had died of an unexplained illness while he was still in medical school. After that, he had buried himself in his work and seemed uncomfortable in most social situations. Past 60, with long white hair and silver bifocals, Josh was rather frail looking—especially since he had developed cancer a few years back and had undergone several operations. But he still carried himself proudly and looked distinguished.

There were only two places where Josh seemed to act confidently and openly. One was in his medical practice, where donning his white coat seemed to give him a definite role to play: the dedicated and competent physician. In his office, Josh was friendly and warm with people and every one of his patients knew he really cared about him or her.

The second place Josh was free was in church. He loved music so much that when he immersed himself in it he seemed to lose most of his self-consciousness. Unfortunately, his love of music was not shared by many others in the congregation, but this did not deter Josh. In church, where he had become the hymn leader years before, he found a captive audience for his only passion. Josh was a terrible leader of song, however. Although he had a beautiful tenor voice and knew and loved the best of both the newer and the older church music, he could never transmit his enthusiasm to the rest of the congregation.

It was Josh who had spotted and developed Molly's love of music. The doctor had encouraged her as a teenager to continue with lessons and had advised her to major in music in college. When she thought of quitting in her senior year after her parents' death, it was Josh who convinced her to continue, even helping with her tuition. The two saw each other often at choir practice (which consisted of the two of them) and would occasionally travel together to Green Bay for a concert. Josh had a great classical record collection and he would often len Molly the albums she could never afford to buy herself but treasured nonetheless.

Maybe it was the differences in their ages, or perhaps just their proven integrity, but their close relationship escaped the gossip so common in small communities like theirs. They would practice their hymns sometimes late into the evening, linger over a cup of coffee at the diner, or even take day trips together without raising one eyebrow in the town.

Although Molly was delighted to see Josh chatting with Pastor Brooks when she walked into church that morning, she would never dream of hugging or even affectionately touching him. Such a display was not part of their relationship. Indeed, the entire town exhibited the effects of its German and Scandinavian roots. It wasn't that people here were cold or unfriendly; quite the contrary. There was endless socializing and neighborliness—but always at an acceptable distance.

So it was at a distance that Molly smiled when she saw her friend and said, "Welcome back, Dr. Josh. How are you feeling?"

"It's been a long winter, but I do believe spring has finally arrived," Josh, with a tilt of his head and a touch to his glasses, greeted her.

Molly and Pastor Brooks smiled at each other. They often kidded Josh about his unfading optimism.

"Oh, sure, you think the old Doc's prognosis is overly optimistic," Josh declared authoritatively,

"but just you wait and see. The snow and cold weather are gone until next November."

"Don't put your snowblower away just yet," Molly responded playfully. "You may just need it one more time."

"People seem late this morning," Josh said, looking around the slowly filling church.

"They're probably caught in the snow storm that developed since Molly walked in," Pastor Brooks said as he finished preparing the altar. Josh smiled, and only shook his head.

The pastor began to move to the back of the church. Josh called after him, "Pastor, can I have a few minutes at the beginning of the service? I want to practice a new song with the congregation."

"Sure," the pastor said. "I don't feel real prepared today. Perhaps you can conduct the entire service."

"No, five minutes will be fine," Josh replied.

As the pastor continued to busy himself with preparations, Molly sat down at the organ. "How are things at home?" Josh asked.

Molly knew immediately what he meant, and her shoulders sank. "The same," she replied with discouragement evident in her voice.

"I thought so much about it while I was in the hospital," he said. "I was hoping he'd stop. He's too good a man not to see what he's doing to you and your family. I know he'll come to his senses eventually."

"Yeah," Molly said sarcastically. "And maybe the congregation will sing today too."

It was a joke between them—but a painful joke. It was hard for the two of them who cared so deeply for music to lead a congregation where no one would sing.

There were a few women in church who sang softly, but Molly and Josh wanted more, much more. They wanted people to experience the richness of music as they knew and loved it.

But people here were as quiet and reserved in their worship as they were in public expressions of emotion. Some women didn't like to call attention to themselves. Some men believed that singing—especially in church—didn't fit the image of a man. Most felt that the music should be left to the pros.

"Maybe today they will," Josh said with a strange, strong conviction. Molly smiled at him but could say no more as she needed to begin playing.

When the time arrived for the service to start, Pastor Brooks nodded to Josh to practice his new song.

Josh walked to the front of the church and Molly could almost hear the collective groan as he reached the front. They hated going over a song that just Molly and Josh were going to end up singing anyway.

"I think I'll start today by telling you a story about a friend of mine," said Josh. "He was a newly married psychiatrist who was trying to establish a practice in a new town. He was doing a lot of public speaking so people would become familiar with him. One night he was to speak on marital communication and conflict resolution and he was embarrassed because he really didn't feel like an expert.

The night before, he and his wife had had an argument where he didn't feel he had represented his profession very well. So when his wife asked him what he would be speaking on he told her the relationship between human development and a merry-go-round. That night he gave the talk. "The next day a woman came up to his wife, who had not attended the speech, and told her how much she had learned from her husband's talk.

"'Listen,' the wife told the woman, 'I've been on that merry-go-round with him a number of times and watched him go up and down and when he finally gets off he's dizzy and sick.'"

This time people did groan, but it was an affectionate laugh for they all knew Doc Josh's jokes.

"There are two parts of that story that are relevant for me today," Josh continued, "One is that I, too, am about to talk about something on which I don't consider myself an expert and I'm uncomfortable discussing.

"Which leads to my second lesson: both the psychiatrist and I would have been better off to be honest in the first place.

"So I'm going to be honest right now about some things that we all know anyway. First, I hate being up here. You know I don't like talking to groups. Fears are often stupid and mine are no exception. I've known many of you since I slapped your bottoms the moment you were born. You saw my face even before your mother's.

But I'm still scared to speak to you collectively.

Try to figure that out!

"But I also hate being up here because this seems like a confrontation between us and I hate confrontations even more than public speaking. You all know I want you to sing and I know you don't want to sing. It's like when I try to convince my patients to stop smoking and get more exercise. I usually lose those battles too." Again the congregation laughed.

"While I was in the hospital this last time I read the Bible some. One of the things I noticed about so many of the miracles Jesus performed was that he seemed to do them for people who were persistent in asking. Today we'd call those people 'assertive'. He helped the people who wouldn't be quieted by the crowd or didn't let the apostles push them away. Occasionally, he'd even make the petitioners take part in their own cure by washing out their eyes or ears in a river.

"I've wanted and prayed for a miracle too, but maybe I haven't done my part. Maybe I haven't been 'assertive' enough. Which reminds me of another story.

"Once there was a holy man who lived in a valley in the mountains next to a river. After a big rain the river flooded. The water kept getting deeper and he kept moving to higher ground. People would come by in boats and ask if he wanted to be rescued, but he kept saying, 'No, God will save me'. Finally, water went over the top of the mountains and the man drowned.

When he went to heaven he asked God, 'Why didn't you save me?' God said, 'I tried. I kept sending you those people in boats!'"

Again the congregation laughed, for they truly loved this old man. Josh turned to Pastor Brooks, who was patiently waiting to start the regular service. "I didn't mean to go on like this," he said. "I've never felt comfortable up here before, but all of a sudden I'm enjoying myself."

"Continue," said the pastor. "This is the best homily they've heard in a long time." Again the congregation laughed.

Molly sat at the organ and wondered when was the last time such a light atmosphere had existed in the church. Josh said, "Thank you, Pastor," and continued.

"Again, there are some lessons in that story for me.

First, if you compare my life to those mountains, the water is just about over the top and soon I'll get a chance to ask God about my miracle. You see, they told me at the hospital I've got less than six months to live, and I just don't have much time anymore to accomplish what I've set out to do."

The congregation gasped. Molly raised one hand to her mouth and the other hand fell onto the organ keys. A discordant note immediately filled the church.

Josh, ignoring the sound, continued. "I think it's something we all knew but were afraid to talk about, but that's not my point anyway. The miracle I want is not to be saved from dying. I'm old and tired and don't need to be saved from that. What I really want is for you to sing. And I won't have to ask God why He didn't grant my miracle, because I know what He'd say." Josh was talking rapidly now, and there was no self-consciousness left. He was confident and he knew they were listening.

"He'd say, 'I placed you in front of those people week after week. Why didn't you take the risk of just asking them to sing? And if they didn't do it at first, why didn't you cry out all the louder?'

"You people are my lifeboats," Josh said, "and now I'm asking you: will you sing?"

There was silence in the church. Most people had their eyes down. Molly looked straight at Josh.

"You know what's so amazing?" he continued.

"I always pictured my needing to get angry in order to ask or demand that you sing, but I'm not angry now. I'm just more aware than ever how deeply I love you people. At this late date, I'm still learning that love can mean other things besides acceptance. Love can mean actions too."

Josh kept going. Molly thought he had forgotten all about time or the Sunday service.

"But don't just sing for me because I'm dying," he said. "Sing for yourselves. Sing to overcome the wasted moments spent worrying about what others might think of you. Sing for your very lives so that you don't waste them as I wasted mine waiting for a miracle. Sing so you'll have the courage to make your own miracles.

"Fathers and mothers, sing to show your children it's okay to be a little crazy; that, as a matter of fact, it's a necessity to survive in this world. Kids, sing to break out of the prison of being 'cool' or 'hot' or whatever temperature you're supposed to be these days. Sing to break free from the rules that tell us how to dress, how to act, and to whom you can or can't talk.

"But also sing to be part of my miracle. Because I have come here today, not because I'm near death and want my hand held, but because I'm alive and I want that to mean something.

"I have come here today to create a miracle and to watch it unfold. And—like the blind man of the Bible story—I will not stop crying out until my voice is heard.

You may not think that your singing is much of a miracle, but I promise you, seeing you at this moment stand up and part your lips and sing would be no less gratifying to me than what Moses must have felt when he saw the parting of the Red Sea.

"It is time to stand up and find your voices, and stand up and use your voices from now on for what is good and right in your lives. Pull out your hymnals. I've chosen a special new song for you, called *Be Not Afraid*. I lied. It's not new. You've heard it before. But this time I want you to sing it, not listen to it. I didn't know how fitting it really was till just now. Sing your hearts out. Don't worry, God can handle the shock."

Josh sat down. It was over. Molly began to play the prelude of *Be Not Afraid*. She looked at the congregation.

Most seemed too stunned to think about anything at all, much less their own discomfort. At the proper moment she began to sing:

"You shall cross the barren desert, but you shall not die of thirst . . ."

A few of the parishioners began to sing softly, while others looked around nervously. The soft sounds encouraged Josh, but he wasn't satisfied. From his place in the front he yelled, "That's a good start but I won't be quiet until everyone is singing."

". . . you shall wander far in safety though you do not know the way . . ."

Several more voices joined in the singing. As Molly played, she wondered how long it had been since any of these people had sung outside their showers.

But they sang, and to Dr. Joshua Krueger, they had the voices of angels. Tears poured from his sparkling eyes.

He left the front and danced among them, shaking hands, picking up children and twirling with them down the aisle.

"Louder!" he shouted, and he raised his arms to direct them. Never had he shown such animation.

The people began to lose some of their own inhibitions as they were caught up in his enthusiasm. They raised their voices higher, and what they lacked in quality they made up for in quantity and volume. Molly pulled out all the stops on the organ, but the people's voices continued to drown it out. Then came the antiphon.

"Be not afraid. I go before you always."

She was sure the church would soon crack down the middle-from the shock, if not from the sound. The people had joy on their faces. Some were holding hands.

In some of the pews the people were actually swaying in unison with the music. Miraculously, when the song finally ended people actually appeared disappointed.

The church was in complete disarray. Fr. Brooks had forgotten to start the liturgy. But it was of little importance, since Josh immediately yelled from the back of the church: "One more time—from the beginning!" Molly started the song all over again.

Josh continued to dance and sing, hug embarrassed parishioners and kiss babies. Finally, with a child on each arm and tears in his eyes, he appeared back at the front of church as the song ended for the second time.

"There is no happier man on earth," he said simply.

During the rest of the service the hymns continued and the congregation sang with zeal.

At the end, no one left. They all stayed to talk—to each other and to Josh. They always stayed to talk but today there was a difference. As a matter of fact there were a lot of differences. They talked louder. They stood closer to one another. They were even touching. Not just by accident, but reaching over to touch a hand or an arm in mid-conversation. It was almost like a drunk, touching for blind companionship's sake on New Year's Eve. But these people were standing straight up, eyes clear and looking straight ahead.

• • • • • • • • • • ● • • • • • • • • • •

CHAPTER 2

THE FIRST ONE TO LEAVE the church was Molly. She didn't stop to talk to anyone.

She left as if on a mission. She went straight home. She didn't stop at the bakery as she normally did. She walked in the door, took off her coat, and went into the kitchen where she found her eldest daughter, Bobbie.

"It's a beautiful day," Molly said. "Why don't you take the kids to the park?"

"Mom, there's still snow on the ground," Bobbie protested.

"Well, what about sledding?"

"They're tired of sledding."

"Well, then, take them for a walk!"

No more explanation was needed. It wasn't Molly's words; it was her voice. Bobbie gathered the two youngest children together and bundled them up and they were gone quickly and quietly. Molly thought of Scott and Ryan, who were still sleeping, but decided to leave them be since this time would be different: no yelling, just a quiet talk. She poured two cups of coffee and carried them to the bedroom where Hank was sleeping. She woke her husband.

"Morning," she said. "How did you sleep?"

Hank's eyes opened slowly. Although he was now almost fifty, his face still maintained a certain boyish charm. His eyes this morning, however, were clouded over like they always were after a night of drinking.

"I was doing fine till just now," he said. She handed him the coffee and sat on the edge of the bed.

"Hank, I want you to quit drinking," she blurted out.

"Does that mean I shouldn't let that coffee you brought me touch my lips?" he asked wryly.

"You know what I mean," she said.

"What brought this on all of a sudden?" he asked.

"It's not all of a sudden," she replied. "I think of it almost constantly. I've just not mentioned it for a while, that's all."

"Then why are you mentioning it now?" he asked angrily.

"I just don't want to spend the rest of my life with you yelling at the children and passing out on the couch every night," she answered.

"Well, I don't want to spend my life living with a holyroller organist either," he snapped, "but that's what I'm doing."

That startled Molly and she retreated inside herself for a moment. She just wasn't good at this sort of thing, but she had to keep trying.

"Hank," she said, "I don't want this to be an argument. That's why I don't bring up everything. I just want you—all of you. I'm tired of competing with the bar and alcohol."

"Well, jump into bed here, and I'll give it my best shot," he said playfully, and pulled her by the arm.

"No, Hank. Be serious," she said, pulling her arm free and raising her voice.

"You know," he said, "that's your whole problem: you always want to be serious. You never want to have any fun, particularly in the bedroom."

"In the first place," she said, "I have too much on my mind lately to have fun. And in the second place, maybe if I had a husband who wasn't either at the bar or drunk all the time I would be interested."

"The thing I'd like to do with you now would take more than my quitting drinking to get you interested, Saint Molly!" he fired back. She knew what he was implying, and now she was angry.

"How would you know if I was interested or not?" she said, her eyes welling with tears. "You're usually too drunk to care."

Hank didn't say another word. He slowly got up, dressed and left. He didn't say where he was going; but then, she knew anyway.

Molly lay on the bed and cried. She had allowed herself once again to think that things could change. She had let herself become excited and she knew better. Now reality came stumbling back in on her and she was angry. Angry at Josh for making her believe she could make a difference, angry at Hank for his drinking, and angry at herself for allowing those painful feelings to take her on another roller coaster ride.

By the time Bobbie had brought the younger children back, Molly had dried her eyes. No one asked what had happened and she didn't volunteer any information. She was soon lost in the little obligations of the day. Scott and Ryan woke up fighting and the little ones clamored for her attention. Hank did not come home till suppertime. He was drunk, so dinner was quiet. The day had changed from warm and sunny to cloudy with light snow. When dinner was over Hank yelled at Ryan for not shoveling the driveway, then promptly fell asleep on the couch. Molly went to bed early, a little more aware of the depression she usually called "being tired" and angry at herself for recognizing it.

• • • • • • • • • • • ● • • • • • • • • • •

I₁ WAS TWO DAYS BEFORE Molly saw Josh again. They always got together at midweek to go over the hymns for the Sunday service. They started as usual, each hesitating to speak what was really on his or her mind. Molly knew Josh was disappointed that she hadn't shared the joy of the past Sunday with him. After all the times they had commiserated together about the absence of singing in the services, he finally got the people to sing and she had rushed off without a word. Three days later and she still hadn't even mentioned it!

But Molly knew she couldn't talk about it without revealing her own disappointment about Hank. So they continued to talk about next Sunday's music with no mention of his victory.

But Josh had changed. He was not as predictable as he had been and without warning he asked, "What's the matter?"

"What do you mean?" she asked. She knew it was a waste of time to hedge now that he had brought it up, but she needed time to think. He was sarcastic, another surprise.

"Oh, I don't know. The fact that I'm dying, the fact that we witnessed a miracle together—I thought you might want to comment briefly, before it was business as usual."

Molly started to cry. For the first time in their long relationship, Josh reminded her of her husband. She saw him as blaming, self-centered, and self-pitying all at the same time.

Still, in spite of her anger, she immediately felt relieved because she thought that he had given her a way out.

"I thought I was special to you," she said. "Why didn't you tell me first?"

He came to her and put his arm around her as she cried.

She felt relieved. Maybe he would let her off the hook.

"You know," he said, "for my whole life, what you just did would have left me apologizing all over myself. But, too late, I'm learning to go with my instincts: that's not what is really bothering you, is it?"

She felt betrayed, but she wasn't sure whether to be angry at herself or at Josh. She chose Josh.

"Let's just say your advice in church is not as sound as your medical advice," Molly snapped. "You should be more careful about getting people's hopes up."

Molly felt nervous and defensive. The thing she had always liked best about Josh was that he never pressed her. Now he seemed relentless. She feared she would never escape until he had read all the pages of her soul. Sure enough, he continued.

"Molly, I know and love you," he said. "You can't hide from me or push me away. But I don't have the patience I used to have, either, because I don't have the time for it now. So why not stop playing these defensive games and tell me what's going on with you?"

His voice sounded harsh and impatient, like Hank's. But his eyes showed love and he was only asking her how she felt.

She started to laugh.

"You know, for a moment there I thought I was arguing with my husband," she said, "but I just realized you're playing my part."

He looked at her strangely.

"Never mind," she said. "I thought after last Sunday that I could go home and ask my husband to quit drinking, just like you asked the congregation to sing. But it didn't work. I knew if I started talking to you about what happened Sunday, you'd know something was wrong. I didn't want to tell you about it."

"I'm sorry about your disappointment," he said, "but please don't run from me now. If you don't need me, I sure as heck need you."

"I'm sorry, Josh. I wish I had more to give you right now."

"You know, part of your problem is you don't have death on your side the way I do." Now it was her turn to look at him strangely.

"You see, one of the reasons I had the courage to ask what I did on Sunday is because I'm dying. Death not only gave me the courage to ask, but it made it impossible for them to refuse."

"What should I do?" she asked. "Hold a gun to my head and say to my husband 'Quit drinking or else?'"

"No," he said, "but there are things other than threatening death that have power. I've asked you when we discussed this before . . ."

"No," she said. "I won't see a counselor."

"I don't blame you," he said. "We're a lot alike, you and I.

We probably find it easier to love things that don't love back like music. Music sits, ever patient, waiting for us to sing or play it. Your organ never asks to be tuned, my songs never demand that I sing them a different way.

"But if your husband quits drinking he may ask you for things, and then you'll have to respond—one human being to another."

Molly didn't like the new Josh; she was sure of it now.

"You don't understand at all, do you?" she cried. "If you did, you'd know that what you say isn't true."

"Then prove it," Josh said. "Go see a counselor.

If you go, and your husband still refuses help, you can truthfully tell yourself, 'I've done all I can.'"

Now she was truly hurt inside. How could anyone ask her to do more! "You know for years how I have struggled with Hank, with my family, and even with my God about this problem. I've raised five children by myself for the last several years. I've had a husband who, at his best, was absent, and when present, added to the problems. How can you dare ask me to do more?"

"Did you ever stop to think I'm not asking you to do more?

I'm encouraging you to get some help so you don't have to do it on your own anymore."

"No," Molly said. "I never once thought of this as encouragement." She gathered her music and stormed out.

Josh hung his head after she left, as if his worst fears had been realized.

• • • • • • • • • • • ● ● ● ● • • • • • • • • •

SHE WONDERED AS SHE PICKED up the phone that night whether it had been Josh's intention to get her mad enough to call. If it had been, he had gotten his way. She hated herself for thinking it, but she hoped Josh lived long enough for her to tell him that the counseling had failed.

"Alcoholism Treatment, Jack Peterson speaking," a voice said at the other end.

"I'd like to speak with a counselor about my husband's drinking," said Molly.

"Would this be just for yourself, or would you be bringing your husband or family with you?"

"Just for me."

"Would you need a daytime or evening appointment?"

"Evening."

"How about Thursday at six o'clock?"

"That will be fine." Molly gave her name and wondered what she would tell the children.

When Thursday came she asked Bobbie to make dinner and watch the children and said she had a doctor's appointment. She left early and drove around until it was time. As she drove, she thought how she might explain her situation to the counselor. The more she thought, the more jumbled her thoughts became.

The counselor's office was at the treatment center outside of town, but she still worried that someone might see her. She parked at the back of the lot and waited until the lot was empty before leaving her car.

She was glad there was no one in the waiting room and the counselor was waiting for her. He was younger than she had expected, which made her all the more confident that this was a waste of time.

"Mrs. Brandt?" he asked as he extended his hand. She answered, "Yes," as her cold wet hand found his warm one.

"I'm John Peterson," he said, "but please call me Jack."

He had an open, friendly face, a shock of dark black hair that fell onto his forehead, and a way of looking straight into her eyes that Molly found disconcerting.

They went into his office and sat down. He looked at her and asked, "How can I help you?"

"As I mentioned on the phone," she said formally, "I want to talk about my husband's drinking."

"What is your problem with his drinking?" he asked matter-of-factly.

She didn't like the reference to "her" problem with Hank's drinking, but she let it pass and answered the question.

"Well, it takes him away from the family so much," she explained. "And when he is home and has been drinking, he is usually sleeping or fighting with our son or me."

"Have you spoken to him directly about it?"

"Yes, just the other day. But my doctor said that there are ways you can teach me that might have more impact."

"That's true," Jack replied. "But first we have to be sure that your husband really has a problem with chemicals. So far, you've only told me he spends a lot of time out of the house and fights with you and your son. I have two questions. One: why do you think these problems are related to alcohol? And two: can you give me specific instances when these problems occur and the role alcohol plays?"

Molly grew silent. She was only partly thinking about his questions. Another part of her was busy resenting the fact that this counselor was unwilling to believe that she knew the man she had lived with for the last twenty years.

"I know these are hard questions," Jack said. "And perhaps you feel resentful that I don't seem ready to accept the fact that your husband has a problem. But distrust of you is not my reason for asking."

Molly was still silent. It was difficult for her to be around people who seemed to know her feelings. Especially when they were as willing to bring them up as this man and Josh were.

"Why should I trust your judgment when you don't seem to trust mine?" she asked.

The counselor sat back in his chair. He didn't seem insulted or hurt, just pensive.

"Perhaps we can look at it this way," Jack said. "You came to me for new ways to convince your husband he has a problem. Part of that process is collecting information you can present to him. Think of what you're going through now as a process of collecting information in your mind and also as practice in presenting it to him."

Molly felt a little better. She still was doubtful that this would do any good, but it was nice to speak to someone who listened to her and whose answers made sense.

She sat and thought for a while longer. Finally she began to tell him how the relationship between Hank and her had changed over the years and what she thought Hank's drinking had to do with it. With Jack's help she was able to identify several aspects of his drinking that—at least in her mind—made it obvious Hank was no ordinary social drinker. After a while, Jack stopped her.

"I think we have enough data to indicate we ought to proceed," he said. "We can look at more of your life at the next session if you decide you do want to go through with an intervention."

"What's an intervention?" Molly asked. Jack sat forward in his chair and his voice softened.

"There is a good chance," he said, "that, based on what you've been telling me, your husband has the disease of alcoholism."

Molly started to protest. Jack raised his hand, stopping her.

"I know you're going to tell me he can't be an alcoholic," he said, "because he goes to work every day and is a good provider. But alcoholism has stages—like most diseases. The purpose of doing an intervention is to stop the progression of the disease before it reaches the stage where he has destroyed his life and his family's. But whether or not he has the disease is not as important right now as the fact that we both agree he has a problem and needs help."

Molly thought for a while and agreed.

"What do we do next?" she said.

She was ready to hear more, but what came next dampened what little enthusiasm she had.

"You need to ask your family—and maybe some others outside the family who are close to your husband—to come with you next time."

Molly's mouth dropped open.

"What do they have to do with all this?" she asked with irritation.

Jack sat back in his chair. The calm, patient look she would get to know well spread across his face.

"If, in fact, your husband is an alcoholic, one common symptom of the disease is denial," he said. "One person is usually not able to break through that denial, especially not his wife who he has learned to tune out over the years. It takes either a crisis or several people telling the alcoholic the same thing at the same time to get through that wall. A family intervention combines both. The crisis for the person is seeing his loved ones all gathered together to tell him how they feel. And, the family and friends all telling him the same thing gives him a message that's difficult to deny."

"So that's what Josh meant," Molly said to herself.

"What?" Jack asked.

"Oh, nothing," Molly said. Her only thought now was to get out of there. The thought of the whole family sitting in one room, confronting her husband on his drinking, was terrifying. Once again, Jack seemed to pick up on her feelings.

"I know it must be scary to think about this," he said. "But remember, alcoholism is a progressive disease.

It's going to keep getting worse. Sometimes after another promise it may appear better for a while, but as long as the drinking continues it never gets better. The alternative is to watch your husband slowly get sicker.

"And your family will go right down with him, because we see every day that alcoholism is a family illness."

"I'll have to think about this," Molly said as a polite way of ending the conversation.

She got up abruptly and extended her hand. Jack got up slowly, trying to make eye contact, but Molly felt his gaze and looked away. He gave her a packet of information to read.

"This should tell you more about how an intervention works. Call if I can answer any more questions about the process. Meanwhile, here's a brochure with the phone number of a local Al-Anon group. You may need some support in working through this crisis, and this group will give it to you." Molly left quickly. She found herself taking in a deep breath of the cold night air, hoping it would cool the fire in her stomach. Instead, it sent a shiver down her back. She shook all the way home.

Afterward Jack walked into the office next door when he saw the door was open and talked with his supervisor.

Rosemary was a pleasant looking woman in her fifties. She had a round face and eyes that sparkled with a little bit of mischief and a laugh that matched.

Jack always like to discuss the cases that he felt were less than successful, to make sure he had done all he could.

Usually, Rosemary reassured Jack in her kind and gentle manner that he'd done what he could and reminded him why the serenity prayer was so popular among those who worked with alcoholics. Sometimes as they were finishing up she would smile and recite it: "God grant me the serenity to accept the things I can not change, the courage to change the things I can and the wisdom to know the difference."

Her eyes were always sparkling with mischief.

. . . .

ONCE HOME, MOLLY WAS HAPPY to see that Bobbie had already taken care of the dishes and gotten the little ones to bed. Hank was sleeping on the sofa. Molly didn't wake him. She just went quickly to her room to change clothes. She stuffed the packet Jack had given her into her dresser drawer.

She thought it would stay there quite awhile before she was ready to look any further into this "intervention" business.

Ryan came home while Molly was changing. He made such a racket coming in that Bobbie looked at him in surprise.

He went quickly into the bathroom and threw up. Bobbie followed him in and shut the door quietly behind her. She put her hand on his forehead and begged him to be quiet as he spit into the toilet. He just groaned, and roared again into the bowl.

Molly ran quickly, still in her robe. She was too late.

Hank had already stumbled drunkenly to the bathroom. He was pounding on the door and yelling, "What's going on in there?"

"Nothing," Bobbie yelled. "Just go back to sleep, Dad."

"Don't tell me 'nothing'," Hank shouted, and jerked open the door.

"What's the matter with you?" he asked Ryan.

"Mush haff da flu," Ryan mumbled as he stumbled to his feet, wiping his mouth.

"You're drunk!" his father answered.

"Takes one to know one!" Ryan replied sullenly Hank was on Ryan in a second and had the boy by the scruff of the neck. The father had had years of practice maneuvering while drunk—a technique at which his young son was not yet accomplished. Ryan was no match for him, and Hank soon had his son's face in his own vomit in the toilet bowl.

Bobbie and Molly rushed to separate them.

"Stop! You'll kill him," they both shouted at once.

"He'll only wish he was dead," Hank grunted. When he let the boy's head up, Ryan was coughing and his face was covered with vomit. Hank's jaw was set. Molly quickly stepped between them with a wash cloth. She looked at Ryan as she wiped his face.

Instinctively, she knew the best way out of this was to support her husband.

"What's the matter with you?" she scolded Ryan.

"I'll take care of him and get him to bed," she said to her husband over her shoulder. "We'll decide on a punishment for him in the morning." She held her breath as she continued to clean Ryan's face.

She breathed again when Hank turned to stumble out of the bathroom.

He turned in the doorway and said, "You haven't heard the last of this, young man!" But he continued out of the room.

Molly sighed. Bobbie followed her father.

Knowing the dance steps to relieve the crisis, the teenager simply agreed as her father mumbled about the disrespectful kids who don't appreciate all that's been done for them.

Molly and Bobbie finally got everyone to bed. They sat quietly for a while in the living room, as if to catch their breath.

In their tiredness they didn't speak, just stared at the empty space in front of their faces.

That was the closest Molly would come to sleep that night.

She lay all night on the living room couch, not wanting to be next to her husband. She kept thinking about the words the counselor had used: "progressive family disease." Even if it didn't get worse, even if he was the only one with the problem, she didn't want herself or her family subjected to it anymore.

In the morning, she woke Bobbie first.

"I know you must be tired, but I need your help. Get the little ones ready for school. I'll try to keep Dad away from Ryan."

Bobbie nodded in agreement and quickly rose to get dressed. Molly went next to Ryan's room. She spoke sternly.

"Ryan, get up for school."

"I'm sick, Mom," was his reply. Now she spoke with fire: "Damn right you're sick. I hope you're as sick as a dog, but if you think you're skipping school, you're crazy."

The boy's feet were quickly on the floor.

Molly then went to wake her husband.

"I'm awake," he said. "You must have gotten up early."

"Yes," she said sharply.

"Boy, you're in a foul mood," said Hank. "What's the matter?"

Molly knew immediately that her husband had no recollection of what had happened the night before.

"I didn't sleep well," she said. She left the room not sure if she was relieved or angry.

When Ryan saw Hank in the hall a minute later, he quickly lowered his eyes.

"Can't you even say good morning?" his father yelled.

"Good morning," Ryan said quietly, trying not to draw any attention to himself.

At the breakfast table Paul, the youngest son, complained of bad dreams. Sally, the youngest of all, missed her mouth with her oatmeal. Everyone laughed, so she did it again. Finally, when they had all left, Molly called the school to say she was sick and would not be in that day. She went to her room and pulled the packet of material from her dresser drawer. She had not expected to look at it so soon.

She first read the material that described the intervention process. It spoke of how the family presents the dependent person with the reality of his or her chemical use.

She read that there would be four sessions. The first would be assessment and education. She and her family would have to talk again with Jack and further convince him that Hank had a problem. They would be taught in the first session how to prepare specific data. That meant they would need to think about specific instances when Hank drank and how it affected them.

In the second session, they'd see a film about an intervention and go over their data with Jack. They would develop a plan to present to Hank if he agreed to get help, and they would discuss their bottom lines, which Molly didn't even want to imagine the meaning of. They would have to decide on the order in which people would make their presentations and where they would sit.

In the third session, they'd roleplay doing their intervention. Finally would come the intervention itself, where they would sit with Hank and present their case to him.

This all seemed so impossible. She was sure the kids would dislike talking and planning without their father knowing it.

She was also sure Hank would have a fit if he walked into a room and they were all sitting there. He would never tolerate listening to the children confront him about his drinking, and he would really be upset if she brought in anyone from outside the family.

She read on. She was supposed to approach the intervention with love and concern and be nonjudgmental. At the moment, though, she wasn't feeling that much love or concern and she felt very judgmental.

When presenting her data to Hank, she would have to talk about how she felt. She had spent most of her married life trying to forget how she felt, and now she was supposed to talk about it.

At the end of the intervention, they were supposed to give Hank options about treatment. How did she know what options to suggest when she herself wasn't sure? There was only one thing that moved her toward the phone, and that was her pain. She was afraid for Hank, but most of all worried about her children. She called the treatment center.

"I wasn't so sure I'd hear from you, especially so soon," Jack said.

"I have some more questions," she said. "Do you have time to see me today?" They made an appointment for later that morning.

CHAPTER **6**

• • • • • • • • • • • ● • • • • • • • • • • • •

MOLLY HOPED THAT JACK WOULD again be waiting when she arrived at the treatment center, but he wasn't. This time she had to sit and wait for him.

It was hard for her because she was so tired of the thoughts that seemed to run constantly through her mind no matter what she did: the thought that her husband might be an alcoholic, the idea that the whole family was sick. These were too much for her today.

But the scene from the night before continued to haunt her: her teenage son drinking; her husband's angry reaction and then his remembering nothing the next day; she herself awake that whole night, then calling in sick the next day. One thing certainly was true: all in the family were affected by Hank's drinking.

Jack finally emerged from his office and she was glad to see him. It amazed her that this person she had only seen once before affected her so strongly, but he did. It wasn't what he said, but the way he listened and seemed to understand.

"Hi!" he said as he came over to shake her hand.

"Hi!" she repeated, and followed him into the office.

"What brings you back so soon?" he asked.

"Well," Molly said, "I fully intended when I left last night never to return, but something happened at home that changed my mind. It made me think that maybe some of the things you said had some truth to them." She related the events of the night before.

"Well," said Jack, "There is no perfect screening test for the disease, but I look for certain clues or symptoms. You describe several things from last night that lead me to believe that a problem exists. Hank's not remembering is an example of what we call a blackout—a loss of memory. The fact that his behavior is very different when he's drinking and that his drinking is obviously getting in the way of his functioning in the family are symptoms of the disease. And all that's from just one incident."

"I was afraid you'd say that," Molly said, "because that leads me to my next question. Is there any way for my husband to get help other than the way you started to describe last night?"

Jack sat back in his chair. "Sure," he said. "There are lots of ways. He may kill someone while driving drunk. He may lose his job as a result of his drinking and quit because of that.

You could threaten to divorce him, or one of the children could run away. But it usually takes some crisis that he can relate directly to his drinking to get him to stop. We call this 'hitting bottom'. It's the point at which the alcoholic finally says, 'I've had enough; I've got to quit.'"

"But I don't want any of those things to happen," Molly said. "Besides, he works for his brother and he's a great worker.

And things would have to get much worse before I'd even consider separation."

"That's just it," Jack said. "An intervention is designed to 'raise his bottom' as we describe it—to set up a crisis that, in the long run, doesn't hurt him or anyone else, yet helps him decide to quit drinking."

"So what do we do, sit around and threaten him?"

"No, that's the beauty of the way we do interventions here.

They work through love, not force."

"Tell me exactly how it works."

"Well, first you must get your family, and perhaps a close friend or relative—the brother he works for, for instance—to agree to gather together and tell your husband how his drinking has affected them. Then each one will tell Hank that he loves him and want him to get help. If he agrees, he'll go right into one of our programs here."

"It sounds so easy the way you describe it; what if some of these people won't be involved?"

"That's quite possible. Often the people around the alcoholic are as much in denial as the alcoholic himself. But it is important for the success of the intervention that at least four, and preferably five, are willing to participate."

A sudden thought entered Molly's mind.

"What if it doesn't work?" she asked anxiously.

"What if all our honesty just makes him angry?"

"Well, there are no guarantees," Jack said, "but we have a good track record. Honesty and risk don't offer any promises, just possibilities and hope. The alternative, though, is to go home and pretend last night didn't happen. That means you live a lie and teach your children to live a lie and ignore reality.

"They will walk around in their private world, distrusting what they see. They will learn not to talk, not to trust, and not to feel.

"Let's not even take last night. When was the last time you or any of your children said 'Dad, why are you so often drunk at the dinner table? Why do you fall asleep on the couch every night? Why does everyone ignore it when you stumble, or when you talk funny?

"Everyone has learned to pretend those things aren't happening. Is that how you want your children to go through their life, Molly?

"I'll bet they've seen you crying after a fight. They may have found the courage to ask, 'Mommy, why are you crying?'

You got angry at them and said, 'I'm not crying,' or, 'I'm not angry.' You're teaching them not only to mistrust their own perceptions, but also that feelings should be denied at all costs."

Molly was shocked and surprised. Was this guy a mouse in her living room? How did he know these things went on in her family?

Whatever the case, when Molly had to choose between honesty and the alternative just presented by Jack, the answer was obvious.

"And even if your husband doesn't agree to go into treatment," said Jack, "through the intervention I think you'll all learn new ways of dealing with your husband's drinking that will help you and your family. It also often has the effect of ruining his drinking now that it is out in the open and he often quits weeks or a month later."

"Okay, okay. You win. Where do I sign up?" Molly said in a combination of terror and hope. Man, she thought, this guy could sell snow in the middle of a Wisconsin blizzard.

Molly sighed. Maybe she'd better check out Al-Anon for some support.

After she left, Jack again went back to see Rosemary. This time he had a number of questions that would involve more than reassurance and even he knew that at one point he had screwed up.

He described to her the incident Molly had described, when Hank had pushed Ryan's face into the toilet. He knew she immediately recognized where he was going. Though it appeared from Molly's reaction that this was the first time such a violent thing had occurred, Ryan was still a minor and this certainly sounded like abuse. This presented a problem to Jack. According to state law, he was a mandatory reporter: if he heard about a case of abuse, he was obligated to report it to the state Department of Child Welfare. He also should have immediately told Molly that he needed to report the incident. But he also knew that if he had, it probably would have threatened their relationship and the trust he was just beginning to build with her.

He also discussed with Rosemary whether he should include the two youngest Brandts in the intervention.

Professionals disagreed whether young children should be included in an intervention. The down side was that there was the risk of intimidation by the alcoholic, and the potential for abuse, especially if the intervention did not end in treatment.

On the positive side, even if they found it hard to articulate their feelings, those tiny faces with tears streaming down them asking a loved one to get help were very powerful.

One of the reasons Jack was so happy to have Rosemary as his supervisor was that she knew everyone. She immediately called a friend in the Department of Child Welfare and explained the situation. He agreed to hold the report while Jack used it as additional leverage—if the intervention itself wasn't enough—to encourage Hank to get help.

They decided also to wait and see on their decision to include Paul and Sally in the intervention until they met them and discovered who else would participate in the intervention.

MOLLY TOLD HERSELF TO WAIT until the weekend, when Scott would be home from college, but what she really needed was the time to rehearse what she would say and build up her own courage.

She thought the best move would be to take the time to speak to Hank's brother, Ken. She knew that would also help build up her courage. Ken and she had been friends since the day they had met. She knew he loved his brother, and, though they had never talked about it, she knew that he, too, was concerned about Hank's drinking.

That's how it was with them: they knew each other's heart without it being spoken.

That's why she knew also where the problem would be in getting Ken involved. Ken had always spent a lot of time with them before he was married. He was Hank's younger brother. He had stayed single a long time, which was one reason he could take the risk of starting his own construction company. He had wanted Hank to go in with him, but by that time Scott had been born and Bobbie was on the way. So Ken went it alone.

Ken was honest and reliable. His business had flourished because people liked him and could count on him. Soon Hank started to work for him as his foreman and that helped, too, because Hank was a better boss.

Although the men liked Ken, they often took advantage of him. Hank let no one take advantage of him or his brother.

But eventually Ken had gotten married and, as often happens, this kind and generous man married a selfish woman.

Maybe that's not fair to her, Molly thought, because Martha does love Ken. She just does it in a possessive and domineering way. She really doesn't want to share Ken with anyone.

At any rate, Molly knew that the only way to get Ken into the intervention was as a package deal: Ken and Martha.

So Molly called Martha and asked if she might come over to visit them that evening. She asked Martha to tell Ken not to mention anything to Hank, and that she would explain why that evening. Martha sounded confused, but agreed.

Molly went to their house after dinner, telling her family she had to practice the organ at church. When she arrived, Ken and Martha had finished eating and were having coffee in their living room. She joined them and tried to make pleasant conversation, but she could see their minds were on why she had really come.

"I know," Molly said, "you must be wondering why I'm here and why I asked you not to tell Hank. I'll get right to the point. I think Hank's drinking has gotten out of hand and I'm seeing a counselor about it. He says the best way for us to help Hank is to get together family and friends who care about him and to have all of them confront him together. Then all of them will ask him to get help. I'm here to ask you if you two would help me with this."

Ken opened his mouth first, but Martha's words came out faster. Her words dripped with concern, none of which Molly believed.

"Molly, you poor dear," Martha said, "I knew that your life was hard living with that man, but do you think it would help if we were there? Hank and I have never been very close and Ken would risk losing a brother and a good employee if this doesn't work."

"I know I'm asking a lot," Molly said, "but there is no other person I'd dare turn to with this."

This time, Ken won and got his words out first. And he spoke with more force than Molly had heard him use before with his wife.

"We would be glad to help, Molly."

He turned to Martha. "But, dear, you're right about you and Hank not being close. I think I should go alone."

Molly fought back the smile on her face as she spoke.

"Thanks, Ken!"

Martha spoke through a tight smile: "Well, Ken, if you think it best . . . But maybe we should discuss it tonight and call you in the morning, Molly."

Molly had a sinking feeling. Leaving Ken to discuss anything with Martha scared her-she knew who would be doing the discussing. But Ken quickly quieted her fears.

"We'll discuss whether it's better for one or both of us to come," he said, "but you can count on the fact that I will be with you for sure and we'll both be there in spirit."

Martha's eyes looked at Ken in disbelief, but her voice said, "Of course you can count on us."

"Thanks again!" Molly said. "Now I'd better be going. I don't want Hank to get suspicious. I told him I was going to practice the organ."

She stopped with her hand on the doorknob.

"I hate this lying," she said in a helpless voice. Then she went on, in a stronger vein. "I haven't even asked the kids yet, but I'm sure they'll go along with it. I'll ask them this weekend when Scott is home."

As Molly drove home she thought, "How I'd like to be a little mouse inside Ken and Martha's house." She knew Martha would have a few things to say. But she felt confident now that Ken would not back down. She knew now also that she could talk to them about the problem no matter how things worked out in the intervention. She was beginning to see what Jack meant about how things would change even if Hank didn't quit drinking after the intervention.

She thought about Josh and about how what he had done was making an impact not only on her life now but perhaps on Ken and Martha's as well. She thought about how she had left him so abruptly a few days before. Perhaps she should stop by and apologize. Then she looked at her watch and decided against it. She didn't want Hank asking questions just yet.

Jack had told her to tell Hank she was going to an addictions counselor, but she didn't want to do that now. She was sure he'd object and, though she felt stronger every day, she didn't feel ready to stand up to him yet.

ON SUNDAY MORNING MOLLY WENT to church early as usual. She was hoping to see Josh, but Pastor Brooks told her he was back in the hospital.

Without Josh there the people still sang, but their voices were much quieter, much less strong.

Pastor Brooks went through the first part of the service with his usual dull efficiency. Molly was praying for strength to continue with this intervention.

It was scary to think of talking to the children—and that was nothing compared to facing Hank. She needed inspiration, but she didn't expect to get it from her pastor.

He was a young man, but old for his years. In many ways, he's perfect for this town. The priest was an intellectual who had studied at the University of Chicago. He had been sent to this parish by the bishop for some "pastoral experience" before he joined the faculty at the seminary.

As he began his sermon, the priest said quietly that he had noticed that the people were singing more softly this morning and that a part of him was glad about that. Molly sank down in her seat at the organ. She didn't want to hear more about singing. She started to tune out and turn inside for strength.

"All my life," Pastor Brooks said, "I have said to myself that what we do doesn't make any difference. It really doesn't matter what happens on this earth, because we are only here for a brief moment. I was never quite sure if my religion made me that way, or if I was taken with religion and became a clergyman because it fit so well with what I believed anyway. 'It doesn't make any difference,' I said to myself over and over. 'It doesn't matter if I'm a pastor or a professor or a bishop.'

"When I'd see people who seemed to need help, I'd say to myself, 'It doesn't matter what I do or don't do. It will all work out according to

God's plan. God will get them the help they need. And even if He doesn't, it doesn't matter because they will probably learn something from their misfortune.'

"Then, last Sunday, I was here when Josh asked you to sing. I had a violent reaction in my stomach. I'm not sure what was happening inside of me, but I know it made me uncomfortable.

That's why there is a part of me that's glad to hear things returning to normal, because I don't like feeling uncomfortable. As a matter of fact, I don't like feeling at all."

Molly sat up straight on her bench.

"As all of you know by now, I like to think," said the pastor,

"and I don't like my thinking interrupted or even stimulated by affairs of the earth. I have all I can do to wonder about the heavens without being bogged down with the trivial human conditions on earth. Last Sunday I was jolted into humanness, a new and mysterious world that I know less about than the heavens. All of a sudden, when I heard Josh talk, it mattered to me that you sang. When I saw people talking, laughing and hugging after church, I was trembling.

What he did seemed to make a difference.

"I thought for a long time about why that was so frightening to me. I came up with three reasons. One, I'm scared to death of closeness. Two, I'm scared to death of feeling. And three, I'm scared to death of the presence of God, Who was more evident to me here last Sunday than He has ever been in my years of thinking."

Molly couldn't believe her ears. Neither could most of the congregation.

"So I'm going to ask—no, plead—with you," the pastor said, his voice trembling with the emotion he tried to hide, "to continue to sing and to ignore the part of me that likes things the way they were. I want you to sing for God, because I hope He likes being present in the way that He was last Sunday. I want you to sing for yourselves, because I think we all need to feel alive. I want you to sing for Josh so that he can hear you in his hospital bed, and I believe he can. But most of all, although it may be selfish, I want you to sing for me. Because even though it scares me to death, I want to feel again, and I know I need you and your voices for that."

Right there on the pulpit, just for a moment, he cried.

Then he caught himself Molly never made it inside herself for inspiration. Fr. Brooks had provided all the inspiration she needed. She thought about herself and her family. She wondered when the last time was that they had expressed feelings, other than anger, to each other. There seemed to be an unspoken rule in the family that didn't allow feeling. But now she felt like changing that and she believed she could make a difference.

For two Sundays in a row now, two usually quiet men of this community had given her a gift she thought she might never be able to repay. But she could play the organ, and they were going to hear it like never before. She announced the next hymn, and played the organ with her body and soul. They both showed through.

It was a joy to play the organ and to get lost in the music and the enthusiasm. It gave her even more of the strength she needed to go home and talk to her family. But she knew they'd still be asleep, so she waited around afterwards to speak with some of the parishioners.

She found out that Josh was indeed in the hospital, but was resting comfortably. For a brief moment she thought about what would happen if she never saw him again but quickly pushed it from her mind. She needed all her energy to be focused on her family right now.

She went home and made breakfast and thought of ways to keep all the children home while Hank went to "church."

It was the family joke that his service started when the bars opened on Sunday. They had breakfast in the usual manner, and after it was finished she announced that the house needed cleaning and all the children were to stay and help. There were groans, but they all stayed—even Scott. Hank soon left, grumbling that "it was about time somebody did something around this house besides me."

As his car pulled out of the driveway, Molly called them all into the living room and asked them to sit.

"What's up?" Bobbie asked. Molly sat quietly for a moment.

"I think it is time that we talk about a few things as a family," she said.

"But Dad's not here," Ryan quickly pointed out. "Isn't he part of the family?"

"Yes," Molly answered, "but he's what I want to talk about.

I think your father has a drinking problem and needs our help to face up to it."

"Mom," Bobbie said, "do you really think Paul and Sally should be involved in this conversation?"

"I'm not sure any of us should be. Dad isn't even here to defend himself," Scott said.

Molly held up her hands and the room was quiet. "In the first place," she told them, "it affects all of us, so I think we all need to be involved. In the second place, Dad will have plenty of time to 'defend himself ' if he feels we are attacking him. But first we need to learn the proper way of telling him how we feel about his drinking."

"And how we going to learn that, Mom?" Ryan asked sarcastically. "Are you going to teach it to us in a song?"

"Don't be a smart ass," Scott growled.

"I wouldn't dare act like you!" Ryan fired back. The two boys glared at one another.

"Why don't both of you pay attention to something besides your petty fights?" Bobbie snapped.

"All right! All of you stop," Molly said firmly. "We would learn how by going to a counselor."

They all sat for a moment frozen. Scott was the first to break the silence.

"That's ridiculous," he said.

"Why do you say that, Scott?" Molly asked.

"In the first place, Dad may drink a little too much," he announced, "but he doesn't have a 'problem,' as you call it.

Second, even if he did, he can take care of it himself and doesn't need us and some counselor sticking our collective nose into his business."

"You haven't been around lately, Scott," Bobbie said.

"Daddy hardly ever comes home sober, and he doesn't even remember the things he says and does. The other night he had a big fight with Ryan and the next morning he acted like nothing had happened."

"The problem is, without me around Dad has no reason to come home sober," Scott said. "The rest of you are just one big disappointment to him."

"My, aren't we Mister Wonderful," Ryan said sarcastically again. "Dad's big hero son that none of the rest of us can hold a candle to. But, then, who would want to? The glare from your ego would blind us! No wonder you don't want to do this thing with Dad. You don't want to tarnish your image by saying anything that might offend your precious father."

Scott glared at Ryan. He looked down at him. He looked down in all ways. He was older, bigger, smarter, even a better athlete. He truly was his father's pride and joy, and he knew it.

"Yes," he said to Ryan, "and you needn't worry, 'cause your image is so far in the sewer you couldn't resurrect it with a diving bell."

With that, Ryan flew across the room at Scott. One quick sideways move and a slight shove from Scott, however, and Ryan flew past, scraping his face on the carpet.

"Stop it!" Molly shouted, as Bobbie rushed to help pick up Ryan and keep him away from Scott. "I have enough problems right now dealing with your father without worrying whether you two are going to kill each other."

"Oh, Ma!" Scott said. "No one is going to kill anybody, and if you worry about Dad it's your own fault. There is nothing to worry about. He's fine."

"That's what I hate about you so much," Ryan shouted.

"You walk around with your head in the clouds. You have no idea what it's like to be a mere human being like the rest of us.

For you life is one big walk in the park, and nothing should bother anyone."

Molly was getting tired. She had not expected the children to be such a problem. She realized that she didn't know them as well as she thought she did. Perhaps she'd been too busy thinking about Hank to notice them.

"Look at all the problems this is causing," Bobbie said.

"Maybe we'd be better off leaving well enough alone."

"But that's the problem: it's not *well enough*," Molly insisted. "This discussion isn't what is causing the problem. It's all the times we all have decided to leave well enough alone to the point where we don't know what 'well' is anymore.

"I'm going to go through with this, and I have already asked Uncle Ken and Aunt Martha to help and they've agreed.

Now which of you is going to join me?"

The room grew silent. The children all looked shocked.

Scott was again the first to speak.

"You mean to tell me that you included Dad's boss in on this crazy scheme of yours?" he demanded.

"Let me inform you that he is first and foremost your father's brother," said Molly.

"But, Mom," Bobbie chimed in, "Dad's not going to like this in the first place, but he will really be mad if we ask outsiders."

"I like Uncle Ken," Sally added.

Paul raised his hand as if he were in school, and, just as in school, no one seemed to notice.

"Dad also knows how to control all of us, and that's why we need outside help," said Molly. "I don't want to live my life in fear anymore and I don't want you children to either. It's time we started acting instead of reacting."

"Where are you learning all these cute little phrases from, Mom?" Scott sneered. "From the same counselor who is teaching you to make a mess of this family?"

Molly looked sharply at Scott.

"If that's the way they teach you to talk to your parents in college, young man, then you can just go back there and stay. I don't have to put up with that."

Scott stood up and said, "And I don't have to put up with this nonsense either!" And he walked out.

Molly took a quick breath. It was rare for her to have a fight with Scott. In fact, he usually related mostly to his father.

If it had been the other way around—if she had the problem— she knew he would have stayed with Hank. But she couldn't worry about that now.

"If anyone else wants to leave this room and not go through with this, now is the time," Molly said. "I'll try not to hold it against you."

No one else left.

"I can't guarantee I'll go through with this, but I'll at least stay and find out more about it," Bobbie said.

"I'll go," Ryan said. "It'll be nice to have somebody else be the center of attention around here besides me."

"I'll go if you want me to," Sally said.

Paul was quiet. But then, Paul was always quiet. Molly was just about to tell them the time and date of the first meeting when he said, "I'll go."

· · · · · · · · · ● · · · · · · · · ·

THOUGH SHE WAS USUALLY WARM and friendly to them, when Bobbie saw Ken and Martha in the waiting room of the treatment center that Tuesday night, she gave them a look that made it clear they should keep their distance. She sat on a chair in a corner of the lobby and never looked up. Molly gave both of her inlaws a hug and thanked them for coming. Ryan gave his usual grunt and sat next to Bobbie. Sally bounced into the room and jumped on her Uncle Ken. Paul slipped in behind her and sat off by himself.

Then they all sat in nervous silence, waiting for Jack to come out of his office. When he finally emerged, the room almost crackled with tension, but, as usual, Jack was softspoken and friendly. His voice sounded almost apologetic as he introduced himself to each of the family members. When he got to Paul, Jack asked him his name as he extended his hand in a greeting. Paul looked at it in shock and disbelief while Jack stood there frozen. Sally laughed.

"That's called a hand, Paul," she said, "and when someone puts it in front of you, you're supposed to grab it and shake it like this."

She stepped in front of Paul and shook Jack's hand.

She sounded as if she were talking to a foreigner who didn't understand the custom. It made everyone laugh as they walked into the office. But by the time each person had found a chair, their smiles had faded and they were serious again. Molly looked around the room into each face. She smiled at each person who was willing to look at her, but most—except for Martha—looked at the floor.

Jack broke the ice.

"Molly, I'd like to know what you told the family to get them to come," he asked.

"Well, basically I said that I thought Hank's drinking had gotten out of hand and that he needed help with it," Molly explained. "I said I didn't think he would get that help on his own and that we needed to convince him that he needed it."

"That's good," said Jack. "Now here's what I would like to do here tonight. First, I want to answer your questions about the process. Then I want you to convince me that Hank has a problem.

"If you can convince me that Hank needs help, then I'll send you home to write down the experiences you can remember—your experiences with his drinking. When you come back, we'll do some planning, and I'll show you a film of another family very much like yours doing an intervention. Finally, on the night before the actual intervention, we'll go through a practice— a dress rehearsal, sort of.

"I always schedule the intervention for a morning, because I'll only do this if the person is sober. It also helps us, since it usually takes a while every day for most of us to get our defenses firmly in place, and that means we'll be more honest and have a better chance of making an impression on Hank."

He looked around the room.

"Any questions?"

"Yes," Martha said. "Can you do the intervention on a Saturday? My husband and Hank work from Monday through Friday."

"I don't usually work on Saturday and I don't like doing interventions then. If working people don't have to get up on Saturday, they stay out late drinking on Friday night—and they may still be drunk on Saturday when we're trying to communicate with them."

"That's no problem," Ken said. "I can take time off, and since I'm Hank's boss, he won't have any trouble either."

Molly saw Martha's face harden, but she remained quiet.

"Speaking of work," Ken continued, "Hank is the best worker I've got. He can work longer and harder that I can. Can he really have a drinking problem if it doesn't affect his job?"

"Well," Jack said, "often a man's job is the last thing to be affected, because it's so important to him. It gives him selfrespect.

A person may lose his house and family, but he makes sure he has a good work record for as long as he possibly can."

"Do you think my Dad is an alcoholic?" Ryan asked. The people in the room squirmed a little, but Jack remained calm.

"Well, from some of the things your Mom has told me, I think that's a possibility," Jack responded. "But that's one of the main reasons you're here now: to determine if your father has a problem. I still need to be convinced."

"I feel as though I'm stabbing him in the back talking about him this way," Bobbie said.

"It may seem that way now," said Jack, "but when your father walks in here, if he does, you will have a chance to be more open and direct with him than you ever have before in your life. And it's important for you to know that you are here out of love, not to hurt or get even. And if you're not, he'll see through it right away, and it won't work."

"But why do we have to do it this way?" Bobbie asked. "It seems so mean!"

Jack looked at the other faces in the room, and he could see the same questioning feeling in them all.

"All right, let me explain," he said. "If your dad has a problem with drinking, one of the biggest symptoms of that problem is that he doesn't believe that a problem exists in the first place. It's called 'denial' and it's part of having what we call the disease of alcoholism, just like having a runny nose is part of having a cold.

"It usually takes some sort of a crisis—some terrible result of drinking, like hurting someone in an auto accident, or losing a job—to break through that denial and show the alcoholic that he really has a problem. What we're trying to do is create a controlled crisis to help your father realize he has a problem— something that will show him what has happened to him without hurting anyone or costing him his job, or his family."

He paused, and looked around at the solemn faces surrounding him.

"But before I answer any more of your questions, suppose you answer some of mine," said Jack. "Maybe we'll decide you don't really need to be here. What makes you think Hank has a problem?"

Ken spoke first, slowly and thoughtfully.

"When I first started the business, Hank and I would stop every night after work at a bar in town. The business was new, and it was fun and exciting to talk over our plans for the future.

I guess I grew up with a notion that it would be fun to stop after work and have a beer with the guys. Our parents didn't drink at all, so I suppose drinking for both of us was sort of a forbidden fruit.

"At first I didn't notice—or care—how late it got, because I had no place in particular to go. Then I began to date Martha and I noticed for the first time that once Hank started to drink, he didn't want to stop. I'd go in for a beer or two, then want to leave, but Hank would try to talk me into one more beer and then one more. If I asserted myself and said I had a date, he'd start making cracks about caring more about Martha than about him or the business. But after a while I realized that Hank cared more about drinking than about me and just wanted someone to drink with. Drinking meant more to him than my company.

"Now I'm here because I want a relationship again with my brother. I'm sure he blames Martha for the fact that we're not as close as we once were, but I feel it's the alcohol that has come between us."

"Very good," Jack said. Then he turned to Martha.

"What about you, Martha? Why are you here?"

"Mostly, I'm here for Ken," Martha said. "I know he'd like to be close to his brother, and misses the relationship they had.

I never suspected the alcohol. I just thought Hank was loud and obnoxious by nature."

Molly looked over at Bobbie. She knew that Bobbie was not wild about her Aunt Martha under any circumstances.

That comment wasn't going to help their relationship. Bobbie looked sharply at Martha, but said nothing.

"It's hard for me to know how alcohol affects Hank,"

Martha continued, "because I've rarely seen him not drinking.

I guess the time I'm most upset about, though, was at our wedding when he got up to make a toast. He not only slurred his words, but he made several lewd comments about our wedding night."

"How did you feel about that?" Jack asked.

"I was embarrassed and humiliated," Martha said with irritation in her voice.

"You may think it strange that I ask you that," Jack said,

"but one of the most important things for you to do when we actually do this intervention is to tell Hank exactly how you feel. Hearing you express the feelings he has caused in you—all of you—will help more than anything else to break through Hank's denial."

Jack turned to Molly next.

"What can you tell me that might convince me that Hank has a problem?"

Molly sat for a moment. At this point she was concerned about the children. How would they feel toward their father after hearing all of this?

"First, let me say that Hank has always been a good and loyal husband, father, and provider. He has never run around with other women, he has never hurt me or the children, and we have never gone hungry because of his drinking. Doing this would be a lot easier if he had. But I think the thing that hurts me the worst is what he seems to have lost because of his drinking.

"Hank never went to college, but he was intelligent. Even though I did go to college, I usually felt inferior to him in a discussion. He liked to read, and we would talk for hours about books we had both read."

Paul and Sally looked at their mother as if she was discussing a man they didn't know. Molly looked back at them and smiled for a moment, but then tears filled her eyes.

"See, that is what is so sad." She put her arms around her two youngest children's shoulders as they sat on each side of her. "You two have never known that man. It's like he's a different person now. It's like there is a vacuum in his head. He says things and doesn't remember them."

"That's what I hate most," blurted Ryan. "That's where most of our fights come from. He tells me I can do something, then when I do it he yells at me because he doesn't remember giving me permission."

"What about you, Bobbie?" Jack asked.

Bobbie looked down at the floor. "Well, I guess dinner time is the worst for me, especially Sunday dinners. I remember a time when my dad stayed home on Sundays. We would sometimes take walks or go fishing. Or Scott and Dad would watch a ballgame on T.V. On Sundays Mom had more time to cook, and we had nice meals that were pleasant. Now Dad is usually drunk when he comes home and any little thing makes him real angry. So we all sit on pins and needles afraid to say or do the wrong thing. I'm so nervous I don't want to eat, but I know if I don't he'll yell about that."

"When I spill my milk he yells," Sally added.

"Not like he'd yell at me if I did it," Ryan added quickly.

"When he yells at you he's smiling, for God's sake."

Everyone looked at Sally's cute face and smiled.

"What about you, Paul?" Jack asked.

"My dad doesn't say much to me," was all Paul could say.

"Maybe that's a problem," Jack said.

Paul looked at him curiously.

"Okay," Jack interrupted. "I think we've heard enough facts to tell us we should continue with this."

He stood up and gazed at them, like a teacher in front of a class.

"From what you've all said I've gathered that alcohol affects Hank's most primary relationships— his family. I've learned that once he starts to drink he can't stop and that his drinking has gotten worse over time. Finally, I've learned that he has memory lapses related to alcohol. There are several aspects of his behavior like the blackouts and personality changes that I look for in determining a problem, but I look for three things that to me are definite indications. One is compulsive use. I don't think Hank decides anymore whether he will stop for a drink after work. I think it is automatic. Second is loss of control. There still may be times when Hank can have one or two drinks and stop, but the point is he can't predict it. I mean, he may go into the bar thinking he will have one or two, but he can never be sure, no matter how strong his intentions may be. Finally, he continues to drink in spite of problems. Even though I'm sure he knows that alcohol is affecting his life, he can't quit.

"That is enough to convince me that he has a problem, that he suffers from alcoholism." He looked into each of the faces before him.

"But it's not nearly enough to convince Hank," Jack concluded. "To convince Hank that he has a problem, we need two things. One, we need specific things he did—incidents where his behavior was affected by alcohol—which in turn affected you. He needs to know about the promises he has broken, the thoughtless things he did or said while drinking, and the things he didn't do because of drinking. Second, he needs to know how that made you feel.

"I want you each to go home and think about these things and write them down. Then I want you to bring them with you the next time we meet. You can set up a meeting time with the receptionist outside. I'll see you then."

They filed out of the office quietly after saying their own goodnights to Jack. They made an appointment for the following week. Ken and Martha left in their car and Molly and the children in theirs. They didn't talk much on the way home. Molly asked the children how they had liked Jack.

Together they murmured, "Fine," but their lack of enthusiasm was heavy in the dark car.

THAT NIGHT, BOBBIE HELPED GET the little ones to bed as usual, then sat quietly in the living room with Molly. Molly knew there was a lot on her mind and gave her daughter time to think, but finally could take it no longer.

"What's up?" Molly asked.

"Mom, I don't think I can go through with this," she said.

She looked relieved to have said it. Molly wasn't surprised.

Molly didn't want to speak too quickly. Since her decision to take this step had been made, it seemed all she had done was sort through alternatives. On the one hand she knew her daughter was important to the intervention, yet she also knew it was time for everyone in the family to start having choices.

For their whole lives, the children had been stuck in boxes:

Scott was the good one; Ryan was the bad one; Sally was the funny one; Paul was the quiet one; then there was Bobbie: she was the helpful one.

Molly knew all she had to do was say, "The children need you," and Bobbie would feel bound to comply. It was very difficult for Molly not to say it. But she didn't. She forced herself to look surprised and say, "Oh. Why not?"

Bobbie took a deep breath.

"It's been hard for me these last few years to maintain any kind of respect for Daddy," Bobby explained. "I've been embarrassed so many times by things he has done and said.

He's never touched me, but when he's drunk, sometimes he says things to me that make me feel like he's talking to a woman at the bar he's just left. Then the next day I see him and sometimes he looks right past me and I know he doesn't remember. Other times he sees me and looks like he wants to crawl into a hole. That's what I'd have to say if I were there, and I just can't do that in front of Ken and Martha and the counselor."

At that moment, Molly hated the world and everyone in it, including the God who had created it. She looked at her lovely young daughter. She wondered if in her whole life Bobbie had ever done anything wrong. It seemed she was born fully grown and had probably worried about causing her mother pain when she had pushed her way out into the world. What had Bobbie ever done to cause anyone pain? Yet here she was, going through this torture. Molly knew the intervention was the only way to end this agony but she didn't have the heart to see her daughter suffer any more. She went to Bobbie and sat with her. Mother and daughter hugged one another as Bobbie sobbed and tears rolled down Molly's cheeks. "You've done enough for this family already," Molly said. "Your youth is enough of a sacrifice. You can skip the intervention. But I'm going to continue so you'll never have to suffer like this again."

"Thank you, Mom," Bobbie whispered, almost out of breath. "And I'm sorry." Molly withdrew from the hug and grabbed her daughter firmly by the shoulders. She looked into Bobbie's sad eyes, still full of tears.

"You have nothing to apologize for," Molly said forcefully.

"You've done nothing wrong and don't ever think that you have."

Shortly after they both went to bed. Molly lay awake and wondered how the intervention was ever going to be successful if she kept losing important people. Bobbie lay in bed with her mother's words running through her mind: "Your youth is enough of a sacrifice." It didn't seem to fit with what she had told her mother. But the confusion and exhaustion of the day finally got to Bobbie and she fell asleep. Molly never did.

Finally, despairing of ever falling asleep, she got up to write down the details Jack had asked for.

At first, it was hard for her. She had spent so many years defending Hank, it seemed impossible now for her to turn around and begin to accuse him—even in spite of what her daughter had just told her. Her first instinct was to excuse him.

She was convinced that things had not been "that bad."

Like most people, she had heard all sorts of horror stories about living with alcoholics.

Molly's own father had often drunk too much and that had been hard on her mother and the children.

But they had all survived. Until recently Hank had been a good father, if not a good husband. Oh, he fought all the time with Ryan—but he often joked and laughed with the smaller ones.

They had always had enough to eat and usually enough money to take care of the demands of raising five children. Except for that recent incident with Ryan, he had never been violent. And he never had actually touched Bobbie; he had just made crude remarks.

No, none of that seemed really outrageous. They were all things that could be explained.

The things that she thought about the longest were the little things—the promises. She thought all husbands had probably promised sometime to be home for dinner by five and hadn't shown up till seven. But Hank had done it countless times. How many times, after the kids had gone to bed, had they argued about it and had he promised to cut down on his drinking and get home earlier? But he hadn't. How many times had he said they'd get away for a weekend, just the two of them? And they hadn't. How many times had they argued in the morning and she thought about the things he accused her of all day long?

How often had she then searched and searched for what she was doing wrong in their relationship only to have him come home in the evening acting as if nothing had happened? Those were the things Molly thought and wrote about. Before she knew it, the room was getting light and it was time to start another day. She thought to herself that this intervention had better come soon or she'd forget how to sleep.

But she had dragged herself through other days, sleepless and worn. Maybe she'd get a nap this afternoon.

IF MOLLY THOUGHT SHE NEEDED any help to get her through the day, Sally took care of that at the breakfast table. Hank asked why no one was home when he had tried to call last night, and everyone looked at Molly. All but Sally.

"We all went to the hospital and talked to some man," she said. When she looked around at the faces that swung quickly to look at her she said, "Oh-oh!" and covered her mouth.

"What man?" Hank asked, and this time all the looks went to Molly. She knew she had to say something, but she wasn't sure if the words were stuck in the lump in her throat or the knot in her gut.

"We went to see a counselor," Molly finally got out.

"What do you mean, 'counselor'? At what hospital? Who's sick?" The questions poured from Hank quicker than Molly could find answers.

She tried to put him off.

"I'll talk to you about it tonight."

"'Tonight' nothing! I want to know now!" Hank said, banging his fist on the table, which bounced the cereal bowls for emphasis.

"Children, you had better leave for school," Molly said, and even though they hadn't finished their breakfast, no one argued. Within seconds the house was quiet and empty except for Molly and Hank. As soon as the door closed, Hank glared at Molly.

"I'm waiting," was all he said.

"We're seeing a family counselor at the Alcoholism Treatment Center." Molly felt like she had squeezed each of those words from her insides. Hank just stared at her for a moment in disbelief. Molly could see his face turn red and was sure his blood pressure was rising. She wasn't sure which of the many thoughts that must be running through his head he would jump on first.

"You bitch," he said. "You're trying to turn my family against me!"

Molly was frightened. He was speaking through his teeth, in hushed tones she had never heard before.

"In the first place," she said, "we are going there for ourselves and not for you. We all need help—someone to talk to about what's troubling us. I think you could use help, too.

"And you don't need anyone to help in alienating your family; you've been doing a good enough job yourself lately doing that in this house."

She saw his face relax just a little and that helped her relax also.

"Just make sure you take care of your own problems and I'll take care of mine," he said. Then—as he always did—without waiting to hear what she might have to say, he got up and left.

Normally when he did that it frustrated Molly, but this time she felt relieved. Rather than think about what had occurred she, too, left quickly for school.

On the way, she stopped at an intersection where she normally turned left. Instead, she did the first irresponsible thing she could remember doing in a long time. She turned right. In the hospital lobby, she phoned the school to tell them she'd be late and then called the hospital to get Josh's room number. She used the back stairs since she knew visiting hours wouldn't begin for hours. Walking down the corridor, she tried to act as if she belonged there. When she was halfway down the hall to Josh's room she heard a voice calling from behind her.

"Miss!" the voice said. She knew instantly it was a nurse calling to her. She ignored it and continued toward Josh's room.

"Miss!" the voice called out again. Again she ignored the nurse and continued to walk. A smile crossed her face. This was twice in one day she was ignoring what she was supposed to do—and she hadn't broken in half. If she could just get a few more feet without the voice overtaking her, she would reach Josh and perhaps he could influence the nurse to let her stay.

By the time she reached Josh's room she could almost feel the nurse's breath on her back. She turned and pushed open the door and there he was. He looked thin and pale but also peaceful.

She stood and gazed at him for just a moment, when the now-irritated voice startled her.

"Miss, visiting hours are not until this afternoon."

Molly turned and looked the nurse in the eye. Her voice was calm but firm.

"I work in the afternoon and have children to attend to in the evening. This man has been my best friend for years and in this hospital almost a week and this is my first opportunity to see him."

"I'm sorry, Miss, but rules are rules," the nurse said. Molly stared at her a moment.

"People are more important than rules," she said, and turned to Josh's bed. She could see his eyes were open and he seemed to be watching with amusement.

"Miss, if you don't leave I'll have to call an orderly," the nurse said.

Gosh, this lady is persistent, Molly thought.

"You'll have to do that," Molly said. "In fact, you'd better get two."

"Nurse, let her stay," a soft voice finally chipped in from the bed. A deep sigh of frustration and resignation came from the nurse.

"All right, Doctor." As she left, she turned to Molly. "I'll be back in fifteen minutes, and then you'll have to go."

When Molly turned back to Josh both of them were smiling. She stood there for a moment just drinking in the peace and serenity this frail man offered.

"You could have spoken sooner," she said with the smile still in her eyes.

"Didn't think you needed any help; looked like you could have had that nurse for breakfast," he said with the smile still covering his whole face.

The room grew silent. The two friends looked at each other and did all their talking in a few brief looks, then confirmed it with words over the remainder of the visit.

Molly spoke first.

"I'm sorry about our last visit," she said. "I still don't know if it's going to help, but we are proceeding with the intervention."

He looked at her and said, "It already has."

She looked puzzled, but thought she understood.

"Yes," she said. "But there has been pain too. Scott hasn't been home from college or called since we've started. It's brought up unpleasant memories for all of us, and we haven't even done the intervention yet. Hank told me this morning that he thought I was turning his family against him."

"Change is difficult and painful, but I believe you are giving your family choices they didn't have before," Josh said.

"I know," said Molly. "I just hope it works."

"I hope so, too," said Josh. "I'll be praying for you. When will it take place?"

"I'm not sure. We still have two meetings before we meet with Hank."

"Molly, I wish you the best." The compassion in Josh's face and voice almost embraced Molly. She stood for a moment wrapped up in it like a blanket. His next statement shocked her out of her comfort.

"It should never have taken this long."

"What do you mean?" Molly asked defensively.

"I should have encouraged you much sooner to do this,"

Josh said, "but so many things got in the way. One was my own ignorance. It's only been recently that the medical profession has recognized alcoholism as a disease, and even now we don't get adequate training in it. It is so different, too, in terms of treatment. Usually we give patients drugs, not try to take them away."

Then there was me and my own feelings. I don't think I've told you how much your friendship has meant to me. You have filled a big void in my life and I was afraid of losing that. I knew I would have to confront and push you in order to make this happen. I was afraid it would end our friendship. I let my personal feelings and my fear of confrontation get in the way of my professional obligations.

"The only thing I regret is that perhaps I allowed our friendship to stop me from pushing you harder to get help and that may have hurt you and your family."

"Time's up."

The nurse stood at the door with an orderly on each side of her. Molly was at a loss. She bent down and gave Josh a quick kiss on his cheek. "See you soon," she said. She left quickly, without looking back.

Molly drove back to school in numb disbelief. She was angry at Josh for misjudging the depth of their friendship. She could think of nothing he could have said or done to her that could have destroyed the bond between them. Why was he so insecure about it?

Yet she also felt sorry that she hadn't told him that. She turned on the radio and sang with the music to drown out her feelings.

WHENEVER KEN WAS WORKING CLOSE to home, he stopped in for lunch. Today he drove up slowly and stuck his head in the door gingerly. Martha had spoke very little to him since the night they had gone to the first intervention meeting. She was sitting on the couch, reading. "Anything for lunch?" he asked.

"Nothing much. I haven't been to the store," she commented, not looking up from her book. Ken sat beside her.

She continued to read.

"What are you reading?" he asked.

"A book," she replied.

"Don't you think this has gone on long enough?" he challenged. She finally looked up from her book, but said nothing.

"You know what I mean," he persisted. "You haven't said ten words to me since we came home the other night."

"I think you're making a mistake," she said, "but I can't convince you of that. So why should I talk?"

"Any time poor Martha doesn't get her way she pouts," he said with obvious sarcasm.

Now Martha threw her book down and glared at Ken.

"My way? My way?" she stormed. "Through this whole thing all I've ever said is, 'Ken, what about your business?' 'Ken, he's your brother.' 'What if it doesn't work?' 'He may never speak to you again.' I've only been concerned about you through this whole thing, and now you say I've got to have my way. That really hurts, Ken." Then she started to cry.

Ken showed no interest in her tears. "You know," he said,

"I've always been afraid that because I give in to you so often you'd think I wasn't a man, but I loved you and didn't want to lose you, so I took that chance. But it surprises me that you think I'm stupid. Don't you think I can see through this phony concern for me?"

The tears stopped. The expression on Martha's face showed rage, then amazement, then slowly softened before she spoke.

"Okay, Ken. The truth is, I don't like your brother and I never have. Even though you have achieved a lot more than he, he still wants to treat you as his kid brother. I'm afraid if this intervention works you'll want to start spending time with Hank and Molly again, and that seems like drudgery to me."

Ken's voice also softened. "I'm sorry you don't like Hank, but he's my brother and I care about him, so I'm going through with this. But I'll understand if you don't want to be a part of it."

"You know," she said, "it seems funny to hear you say you're afraid of losing me, because I'm terrified of losing you. I don't want your brother to take you from me. I don't have any friends.

You're all I have and when you're gone—no matter what I'm doing—I'm thinking of you coming home. You're right: I am selfish. I don't want to share you. I think it would be better if I didn't go to the intervention.

"But I promise I'll give your brother another chance if he gets sober."

Ken took Martha's hand and smiled at her.

"Sorry there's nothing for lunch," she said, smiling and stroking his face, "but it doesn't have to be a wasted trip."

His voice was husky as he said, "It hasn't been." Then he picked her up and carried her, giggling, to the bedroom.

CHAPTER 13

● ●

THE GROUP—MINUS TWO ORIGINAL MEMBERS, Bobbie and Martha— gathered again in Jack's office the next Monday night. Jack set up two films for them to watch. The first was called "The Enablers." It was about a woman alcoholic and her family, but Molly had no trouble identifying with it. She thought to herself how much families must have in common where alcohol plays such a big role. She could even see how some of the patterns in her parents' marriage were repeating themselves in hers. She decided right then that, whatever happened in the intervention, she would join an Al-

Anon group she had heard of and she would encourage the kids to go to Al-Anon or Alateen.

The second film was called "The Intervention."

It showed explicitly how to set up an intervention. When Molly saw the alcoholic walk into the room with all the people waiting, she thought the knot in her stomach would never again come unraveled. She wondered if she could ever go through with this, and, if she did, what Hank would do to them for putting him through it. But the movie ended on a positive note. The alcoholic agreed to go into treatment. Once again, Molly had a flicker of hope.

After the films were over they gathered in the room with Jack. He asked them first how many had written down what they wanted to say. Molly was surprised that she was the only one who had. Jack didn't seem angry or surprised. He simply said, "As you can probably tell from the movie, when the time comes to confront Hank there's going to be a lot of tension.

If you have your statement written out, you'll feel more comfortable. You can refer to it or just read it aloud." He looked at each of them in turn, speaking very carefully.

"We may only have one chance at this, and I don't think you want to lose it because someone is too nervous to say his or her part."

"You don't have to worry about me," Ryan said. "I've been waiting all my life for a time when I can talk and my dad has to listen." Jack smiled, as did everyone else.

"Okay," Jack said. "We have several things to do tonight.

I want to hear what each of you has to say, and give you some ideas about how to say it with more impact. But most of all I want to teach you to say it in a way that won't make Hank defensive. Then we have to decide who will go first, second, and so on. We have to decide on the day and the time of the intervention and how you will all get here. I want the rest of you here at least fifteen minutes before Molly and Hank. The night before the intervention we'll practice one more time. Molly, since you are the only one who wrote anything, let's hear from you first."

Molly was startled. She felt embarrassed to read what she had written in front of the others. She was no stranger to writing; she often had written things in a journal she kept in the "circular file." She'd write her thoughts and feelings down on paper, then burn it or tear it up and throw it away. It sometimes was the only thing that kept her sane. But to read out loud what she wrote—that was another matter.

"I don't think I should be first in the intervention," she said, directing her eyes at Jack.

"I agree," said Jack. "By this time Hank is immune to what you say. But for now, go first."

Molly started slowly. "Hank," she said. "Do you remember when we were first married and we would sit and talk for hours?"

"I hate to interrupt already," Jack said, "but don't start out with a question to Hank. Remember, we want him to listen, not talk. So don't give him the opportunity to take the floor.

Start out with, 'I remember . . .'"

Molly started over, "I remember when . . .," and continued with the many times he had promised to quit and hadn't—how it hurt her to see his sharp mind disappear in the fog of drinking and hangovers. When she had finished, Jack spoke again.

"That was very good, but you need to include more specifics and more about how you feel. Here's a general outline you can use: start with, 'Hank, I love you,' then a description of his behavior. But when you describe it, avoid words that are judgmental like, 'You were drunk.' Just say, 'You were drinking,' or, 'You had had several drinks.' Then describe how you felt.

End by saying, 'I love you,' or, 'I care about you and I want you to get help!' It is also important that you avoid words like right and wrong which also imply judgement. And avoid generalities like 'always' and 'never.' Don't say 'you are always late,' or 'you're never sober any more.' The alcoholic can often come up with just one exception and it makes the statement untrue."

Ryan was the next to share.

"Dad," he started, "a few weeks ago I came home after I had been drinking. You were asleep on the couch and I went into the bathroom and I was throwing up. Mom and Bobbie came into the bathroom to help and we woke you up from your nap . . ." He related the whole incident, spitting the words out one by one. At the end he spoke of being angry and disgusted.

He said he was frightened the next morning of what his father might say but wasn't surprised that Hank didn't remember what had happened.

"That's excellent data," Jack said, "but can you think of how else you felt besides angry and disgusted? You see, if your dad is like other people I've worked with—and I suspect he is—he'll be looking for a way to get the heat off of him. The best way to do that is to get into an argument with someone who's angry at him and who's had a lot of practice arguing with him before. I suspect that's you on both counts."

"But I am angry with him," Ryan protested.

"I know that," Jack said, "and it sounds as though you have a right to be, but what else did you feel when that event occurred?"

"Just anger," Ryan replied.

"Think about it," Jack said gently. "If it had happened to me I think I would have felt a lot of other things, too, but I don't want to speak for you."

Paul spoke next.

"Dad, I love you," he said. "I remember a time when I was small. Ryan had some friends over and they were playing baseball in the backyard.

I wanted to play, too, but they said I was too young and I wasn't good enough. I was crying when you came home and you asked me what was wrong. You came close and I could smell liquor on your breath and when you picked me up we both almost fell over. I told you about what Ryan and his friends had said. You went up to Ryan and made him give you the ball. You kept throwing it to him so hard his hand was hurting and if he missed it you mocked him and said he wasn't good enough to play with you. All his friends went home. I was embarrassed for Ryan and afraid that he would think I had put you up to it.

"I remember another time that Scott had a girl over to the house in the evening. She was real nice and they were letting me stay in the room and talk to them. You had been drinking all day and were in the bedroom, but you came out to get a beer from the refrigerator. You had only your underwear on, but you walked right in front of them and even stopped to talk. You stood with your legs wide apart like when you've been drinking a lot and you swayed back and forth. You slurred your words so it was hard to understand what you were saying. You told me to get out of there because they wanted to neck. I left, but I could see that both Scott and the girl were real embarrassed. I never saw that girl again.

"I began to think it was better not to have friends than to be embarrassed like that.

"I love you, Dad, but please get help." Paul's voice shook on the last few words.

Everyone in the silent room stared at Paul.

"That's perfect," Jack said. Molly thought she heard amazement even in his voice. Paul smiled broadly in a way Molly had never seen before this moment. She asked herself when the last time was that Paul had been complimented and she couldn't remember.

"I'm sorry about the pain you've been carrying around, Paul," Molly told him, "but it certainly is beautiful the way you've expressed it. If I was your father, I certainly would go for help." Paul smiled all the wider.

"That brings up another important point," Jack said. "What happens if in spite of your best efforts here, Hank doesn't go for treatment? You need to think about what you need to do to take care of yourselves if Hank refuses to get help."

"I don't understand." Sally said

"Well suppose your dad picks you up from school one day and as you enter the car you can tell he's been drinking. Do you tell him you would feel safer walking home?"

Molly's heart sank, and she suddenly realized how much she was beginning to believe this would work. Now her old doubts came crashing back. It doesn't take much to cut through hope—it's such a slender thread, she thought.

Ken spoke up first.

"Well, as I said before, Hank is an excellent worker, so I can't threaten to fire him. Our personal relationship has deteriorated anyway. So I guess for me not much will have changed."

"I'll have to think about it," Molly said.

"You wouldn't leave Daddy, would you, Mommy?" Sally asked in a frightened voice.

"No, Honey, I don't think I would," Molly said carefully.

"But we can't continue as we have been, either. I'll have to think about it."

A pained look came over Sally's face.

"Would you like to do yours next?" Jack asked Sally. The little girl still looked sad, but it gave way to a slight smile and a look of importance. "I'm not ready with mine yet," she said.

"I'll think about it and tell you next time." Molly smiled. Jack looked as though he was about to push her to come up with something, when Molly waved him off.

"That's okay," she said. "You can wait, Sally. But make sure you're ready next time. What you say to Daddy is very important."

Finally, Ken read his letter next. His nieces and nephews were amazed by the way he talked about their father. Thank God for Ken, Molly thought. Hank will listen to him if he'll listen to anybody.

Next they talked about what they thought would be best to suggest to Hank as a treatment plan. Jack suggested that, because he worked full time and had a supportive family, they should consider outpatient treatment.

"He will probably need at least three to five days of detoxification to get the alcohol out of his system, but after that he can work during the day and all of you can attend the outpatient program in the evening. If we do the intervention on a Thursday, he can be detoxed through the weekend and return to work on Monday. Then he can start outpatient treatment on Monday night and go to AA meetings on the weekend."

Before they left, Jack took Molly aside and told her about his own bottom line plan—the abuse report that he could use as added "encouragement" if Hank was unconvinced by the intervention. She dreaded what even the threat of being charged with abuse would mean to both Hank and Ryan. But reluctantly she agreed to it as a last resort.

MOLLY WONDERED ALL THE WAY home how she was going to get Hank to agree to go to counseling, especially because things had been better at home since she had raised the subject. He was coming home at night in time for dinner, staying awake after dinner and even helping the children with their homework.

He talked and laughed with them the way he used to do.

A few days passed without her having the courage to ask him. Then the opportunity presented itself. It was the first really warm day of spring. Molly loved to open the windows and let the spring air rush through the house, blowing out all the air that seemed to have been trapped inside all winter long.

Hank was late for dinner, so Molly fed the children and kept Hank's dinner in the oven as she often did. As they were finishing dinner they heard the car pull into the driveway and then a crash. At the noise, Ryan's face went pale. Molly turned to him immediately.

"What's the matter?" she asked, with dread in her voice.

"I left my bike in the driveway," Ryan said. The whole family knew what that meant. Hank had a "thing" about stuff in the driveway. Even when he was sober it upset him, but when he was drinking it became the moral equivalent of an assassination attempt.

"Ryan! Get out here!" he shouted.

"Mommy, I'm scared. Will Daddy hurt Ryan?" Sally asked. Molly thought for a second.

"Ryan, get out here!" Hank yelled again. Molly thought it was fortunate that Hank's concern about the driveway even included her car. She always parked it on the street before he was home, because he told her she didn't know how to pull it into the garage. So she always let him pull in first, then drove hers in later.

"Bobbie," she spoke in a hushed voice so Hank would not hear her through the open windows. "Take my car and take the children to Uncle Ken's house. Go out the front door when Dad comes in the back. Don't come back home till I call you."

"Ryan! I know you're in there!" Hank shouted again.

The kids stood by the front door until they heard their father come in the back. Then they silently left.

Hank had some trouble negotiating the steps and the door into the house, which gave them some extra time.

Molly sat quietly at the table.

"Where is he?" he asked.

"Who?" she asked.

"You know perfectly well who," Hank said. "And where is everyone else?"

"I sent them away," Molly answered.

He looked at her sternly. "I'm tired of dragging things out of you, Molly. What the hell is going on?"

"I sent them away because they're afraid of you when you're like this. And frankly, Hank, so am I," Molly said. She was surprised at the calmness in her voice. She knew that later, when the impact of what she was doing finally hit her, she'd be shaking for hours.

"Well then, they just left," Hank roared. "I'll just go find them."

"If you get in that car I will go right to the phone and call the police. I'll tell them you're drunk and the direction you're heading," Molly said firmly, but still calmly.

She could feel herself shaking inside.

"Why are you doing this to me, Molly? Why are you trying to take my children from me?" Hank asked in a pleading voice that surprised Molly. She realized that he was genuinely confused.

Confused by his own denial. She felt some compassion for him.

"I don't want to take your children from you, Hank, but when you're drinking like this and you get so angry, I'm afraid you'll hurt them," she said.

"Oh, bullshit!" he said. "That's just all the nonsense you're probably getting from that counseling crap." "Why don't you come with me and make sure that they don't brainwash me?" Molly said in as inviting a manner as she could. She was proud of herself for thinking so quickly. Usually she'd think of an idea that good later, and wish she'd said it.

"I'll just have to do that," he said. Then he went back out to the driveway to try to remove Ryan's bike from under the car.

Molly knew that it was Hank's bravado and booze talking. Still, he had agreed and she thought it was enough of a commitment that she could use it on him later. He stayed outside quite a while. Every once in a while she could hear him curse some more. He gradually got quieter, though, and after a while she heard only mumbles.

She decided to go out to him.

"Need any help?" she asked.

"Damn handlebar is caught in the bumper," he muttered.

Together they worked and finally got the bike loose.

Afterward, they went inside and had supper. Hank was quiet during the meal and Molly bided her time. She wasn't sure how much he had had to drink. She had no way of being sure he would remember the conversation in the morning. He seemed calmer, but she knew that the wrong words might just set him off again.

Finally he broke the silence. "Why aren't those kids back yet? Where did you send them—to China?" She wasn't sure what to say.

She finally decided to risk the truth. "I told them to go to see your brother. I told them I'd call them when they should come home."

Molly got up and went to the phone. She called Ken and told him to send the children home. She whispered into the phone, "He's agreed to come. Tell Ryan to apologize to him as soon as he gets home."

THE NEXT DAY, MOLLY CALLED Jack and set up a time for the intervention: eight o'clock on the following Tuesday morning. They agreed to meet the evening before to practice.

That evening, when Hank came home, she gave him time to have dinner and take a nap. Shortly after he awoke, she sat next to him on the couch.

"We're set to go to the counselor at eight on Tuesday morning," she said. She could tell by the look of pain and disgust on his face that it was not going to be easy to convince him to go.

"I can't go then. I work during the day, you know."

"Ken will let you off if you tell him you have a doctor's appointment," she said calmly.

"He's my brother. I'm not going to lie to him—and besides, we're running way behind on the deadline for those new apartments. I can't leave him short-handed like that."

"Then tell him the truth. Or tell him you're going to the hospital for a check-up. That isn't a lie," Molly responded. "I know Ken depends on you heavily, but certainly he can get along without you for a few hours."

She saw him shaking his head and knew she had not convinced him.

"Would you like me to call for you and ask your boss for permission?" Molly asked. She tried not to say it sarcastically, and hoped she had succeeded. But she knew that his pride would not allow this to continue.

"I don't need anyone to do my asking for me," he said. "I can get off if I want to but I don't like to take advantage of my brother that way."

"You are the best, most consistent worker he's got.

You never even take a sick day, even when you're sick." She wanted to say, "no matter how hung over you are" but thought better of it. She was trying to appeal to his pride, not start another fight. Besides, she really was amazed at the discipline it must have taken for him to drag himself from bed on those "mornings after." People who thought that people who had trouble with alcohol were just weakwilled had never seen Hank pull himself out of bed after a night of heavy drinking.

"This is really important to me, Hank. Please call him and ask him." She picked up the phone and handed it towards him.

"I'll ask him tomorrow at work," he said.

"No," she said, "you'll get busy and forget."

He grabbed the phone.

"Oh, all right. God! You've become a nag."

He called Ken. Molly knew right away that Martha must have answered the phone by the coolness in his voice.

Without identifying himself, Hank asked to speak to Ken.

"Ken," he started, "would you please tell my wife that we are too busy right now for her to be scheduling appointments for me at the hospital during working hours?" He was smiling now and was getting ready to hand her the phone when his expression changed.

Molly knew that Ken had caught on.

"But you know how busy we are," Hank said. He was unable to hide his surprise and disappointment that his brother was unwilling to go along with his obvious lead.

"It's Tuesday," he said. "I'll only be away a few hours, I guess." There was a lost puppy tone to his voice.

He handed Molly the phone.

"Okay," he said, "but I hope you're not expecting too much out of this."

A quiet "Thanks, Ken" was all Molly could manage before she hung up.

Now, she thought, if I can just keep this ship afloat through the weekend.

THE WEEKEND PROVED UNEVENTFUL. NEITHER Hank nor any of his children mentioned the intervention, and Hank did not drink at all. Even Sunday services were uneventful, although the congregation did seem to try to sing a little more than usual.

The calm before the storm, Molly thought.

The remaining group gathered in Jack's office the night before the intervention to practice.

"This is our last chance to get our act together before the morning," Jack said. "We have to decide what order you're going to go in. And this time, I'm going to play Hank's role and respond the way he might tomorrow to make it all the more realistic.

"Now, who should go first? It should be someone who has some influence with him."

"Well, that is surely not me," Molly said.

"I suppose I should go," Ryan said with a laugh.

"How about you, Ken?" Molly asked.

"It's probably good to start with someone who's not an immediate family member," Jack commented. "That is likely to have a calming influence."

"Well, if you think it's best," Ken said. "But remember, I'm Hank's younger brother, so don't expect miracles."

"But he respects you and you're his boss," Molly said.

"I know that," Ken said, "but I have to tell him right off that I'm not here as his boss, just as his brother and friend."

"That may make him feel less threatened and more willing to listen," said Jack.

"Well, if that's what you think best, I'll do it," Ken said, "but I don't think I'll sleep too well tonight."

"I think it might also be good if you sit next to him, Ken," Jack said. "I want each person to know where they're going to be sitting tomorrow and we'll only leave one chair open for Hank. I want him to sit by people who can be supportive, but also who can calm him down if he gets upset."

"Boy! you don't leave much to chance, do you Mr. Peterson?" Ryan said.

"Not if I can help it," Jack answered. "There will be enough tension here tomorrow to cut it and serve it up in large slices," he said, "so the more each person is prepared, the bigger advantage we have that it will come off smoothly . . . and that it will have more of an effect on Hank than on us."

"You make it sound as though Dad's our enemy," Paul said.

Jack turned to look at Paul for a moment, then around the room at the rest of the family.

"Based on the data you've given me, I have no doubt that Hank has a life-threatening disease that many people deny right up to the moment when it kills them," Jack said seriously. "No, Hank is not your enemy; the disease and his denial are. We have to get through his denial, or you will all suffer, including him."

Jack was intense as he spoke. Molly hoped that he had made an impact on the children. It seemed so, because they quickly decided who would sit where. They also agreed on the order in which the rest of them would speak—Ryan, Molly, Sally, then Paul.

"I think we're ready to start after two more things are decided," Jack said. "Molly, you and Hank should come together. Alone. Ken, can you pick up the children at school or at their bus stops and bring them here?"

"Sure," Ken replied.

"Good," said Jack. "I'd like you to be here at least 15 minutes before the eight o'clock starting time.

"Second, if Hank agrees to get help you must decide on what treatment you want to insist upon. I think he should go through treatment before attending AA, but he doesn't have to pick this facility. There is one in the next town over. He can also choose between inpatient and outpatient treatment."

Molly spoke up quickly. "I agree that Hank needs treatment, if not for himself then for me. I don't think I would believe he was not drinking if he just attended AA meetings. Besides I think we all need the help that a treatment center can provide. I've learned to feel comfortable here, so let's offer him treatment as an outpatient here."

Everyone quickly agreed, for by now they were all following Molly's leadership. It was a new experience for all of them.

"Now," Jack said, "let's pretend that I'm Hank and that I have just walked in with Molly. He may make a comment or two, but he'll probably be too surprised to say much. After he sits down I will say to him, 'Hello, Hank. I'm glad you could come. These people are here today because they have some things they'd like to share with you. Are you willing to listen?' He will probably agree. At that, I will turn it over to you and it's pretty much your show. I will talk only if Hank gets defensive and argumentative. If so, I'll say, 'Hank, you promised you'd listen.'

"Now I'll put on my other hat and become Hank.

Call me 'Hank' or 'Dad' when you talk to me. It will help you to get more completely into what is going to happen tomorrow."

They started the intervention, speaking in the order upon which they had agreed. Ken went first, and stuck closely to the script he had followed in the earlier practice session. Jack, role playing Hank, made a few comments but mostly just listened. Ken finished with, "I love you and I want you to get help."

"Dad," Ryan said next, "a few weeks ago I came home after drinking. I threw up in the bathroom and Mom and Bobbie were taking care of me, but you had to come in and you seemed worse off than me. You were yelling at me for being drunk and I said, 'It takes one to know one,' and you just stuck my head in the toilet.

If Mom hadn't stopped you, you might have drowned me. I felt so angry at you that I wanted to forget you were my father. The next morning you acted like you didn't even remember."

Molly turned to Jack. She knew that he would start an argument with Ryan and hoped Ryan would see through it. Sure enough, Jack, role playing Hank, jumped on Ryan's comment.

"Well, what are you doing coming home drunk?" he said.

"Imitating you, what do you think?" Ryan answered sharply.

"You think you have permission to act like a smart ass because you have all these people around?" Jack shot back.

"Yes. For a change you're the one who has to take some heat in this family instead of me," Ryan said. "Maybe that's because no one screws up as much as you do," Jack said.

"Mommy, he sounds just like Daddy at the kitchen table," Sally said.

Jack waved his arms. "Wait a minute. I have to speak for a moment as myself. Ryan, remember you can't argue with him. If he hooks you in that way, he takes the attention off himself. You're going to have to control your anger or it would be better for you not to be here. Try starting with some other feelings besides anger. What else did you feel besides anger?"

Ryan put his head down and shook his head. "I don't know. When I think of him I only see red. Besides, even if I could think of other feelings I don't think I trust him enough to give him the satisfaction of knowing. I just don't think I can do this. I'm sorry, Mom."

Molly's heart sank. She looked at Jack.

"Can we do this with only four people?"

"I'd like to have more," he said, "but we've come too far to turn back now. We'll do the best we can. Ryan, you can still help out. I'd like you to roleplay your father for the rest of the intervention."

"I'll try, but I don't know if I can act like him," Ryan said.

"Why not?" said Jack quickly. "You act just like him.

He's angry all the time and so are you."

FOR BOBBIE, THE DAY STARTED out as usual. She dressed herself and then helped Sally get dressed.

"Now you have to be a big brave girl today, okay?" she told her little sister in a soft voice.

"I will, Bobbie," said Sally, "but it would be easier if you would be there."

"Shhhh!" Bobbie put her finger to her mouth. "Daddy doesn't know you'll be there, so we have to keep it a secret till he arrives."

Tears filled Sally's eyes. "What if I make a mistake?" she asked.

"Just do what you can, Honey," Bobbie answered. "No one can ask more of you than that." Bobbie gave her sister a hug and held her for a long time. When she finally let go, Sally seemed to be better. Bobbie put her arm around Sally and they walked down together to breakfast.

Molly was already cooking breakfast. She felt tired, but she was sure the events of the day would quickly cause her to rally. Paul and Ryan soon joined them in the kitchen. They were all sitting at the breakfast table when Hank joined them.

They all looked up quietly as he entered the room.

"Good morning," he said to them. They all sat quietly.

"What's the matter with you kids? You act like you've seen a ghost." His voice sounded irritated. Molly thought quickly.

"They're not used to seeing you at this time. You've usually gone to work before they're even up."

"Yeah, Dad, you playing hooky today?" Ryan asked with a smile. Hank looked back at him like he didn't appreciate Ryan's humor, so Ryan looked down to continue his breakfast.

The children ate quickly and left, and Molly breathed a sigh as they left. She looked at the clock. It was seven fifteen.

She wondered if she could last the next half hour. She went up and showered for as long as she could, then dressed slowly.

She came down and cleaned up the kitchen and still had five minutes to kill before leaving. Hank was still sitting at the kitchen table drinking coffee. He was dressed, but hadn't shaved.

"Don't you think you should shave before we go?" she asked meekly.

"I plan to," Hank said.

"We really should be leaving pretty quick."

"One morning I don't have to go to work and can linger over a cup of coffee, and you've got to rush me." His voice sounded angry. Molly knew he would like nothing better than to get into a fight and then storm out so he could get out of going.

"I'm sorry," she said, "take your time."

He did that. He sipped slowly on his coffee, then took forever shaving, but Molly kept quiet. When they finally left it was almost eight. Luckily the hospital was not far away. Molly knew it would be a quiet car ride. On the way over she busied herself worrying about the children. She wondered if Ken had picked them up and how they were feeling. She even wondered about how Ryan and Bobbie would feel not being there.

Ken had picked up the two youngest children at their bus stop by seven-thirty and was at the hospital by twenty minutes to eight. They all came into the room and sat in their assigned places. The room was as quiet as Molly's car as their eyes roamed from the clock to the door and back to the clock.

When Molly and Hank finally arrived, Molly walked into the room first and sat in her seat, leaving only one remaining chair for Hank. He looked angry and confused. Jack stood up and shook his hand.

"Hank, I'm glad you could come. My name is Jack Peterson and I believe you know the rest of these people. They are here today because they care about you and they have some things they'd like to tell you. Are you willing to listen?"

Hank looked around the room. No one looked at him but Jack.

"I don't like surprises," Hank said.

"I can understand that," Jack said, "but will you listen?"

108 S O B E R S P R I N G

"Yeah, I'll listen," was Hank's gruff reply.

CHAPTER 18

AT THE HIGH SCHOOL, BOBBIE was unusually fidgety in her homeroom. She glared at Tom, who sat next to her. She had been in school with him since grade school and they were exact opposites. She never got in trouble and he was rarely out of it. Their classmates often teased them about liking one another, but Bobbie acted as if she hated him. The homeroom teacher was out of the room, so of course he was acting up.

While she was watching him, he stopped abruptly. When she looked to the front of the room it was not difficult to figure out why. The dean had walked in, and he was a six-foot-two former Marine who looked as if he could have Tom for lunch.

But he called Bobbie to the front of the room and spoke to her softly.

"The homeroom teacher is ill and we're having trouble finding a substitute. Would you look after the class, please?" He really didn't bother to wait for an answer. "Just write the names of those who cause trouble on a list and they'll get a detention.

Take roll and bring any absences to my office on your way to the next class." The dean never questioned that she'd do it, or considered how she'd feel turning in a list of her classmates for detention. This was the reputation Bobbie had at the small high school. She was considered more a peer of her teachers than of her fellow students.

Bobbie looked slightly irritated after the dean left the room, and Tom's immediate talking and laughing didn't seem to help. She tried to busy herself with the roll call, but Tom seemed unwilling to be denied her attention.

"Tom, I'm going to have to put your name on a list for detention," she said. She seemed patient enough, but Tom quickly tested it.

"Go ahead, you snitch," he responded.

"Please, Tom. I have to get the roll done," she said, trying to reason with him.

"Please, Tom. I have to get the roll done," he mocked. The camel's back had been broken.

"Why don't you grow up?" she said in a belittling manner.

"Why don't you grow down?" he said, matching her tone.

She sat motionless for a moment, then tears filled her eyes. She closed the book she was working on and slowly walked from the room, carrying the book with her.

Tom didn't seem frightened for himself when he went after her. He seemed genuinely concerned for her. His voice sounded tender when he reached her and gently grabbed her arm. "I'm sorry, Bobbie," he said. "I guess I don't know when to quit." She didn't pull her arm from his. Instead she turned toward him and touched his face with her hand. With tears still in her eyes she looked right into his.

"You may have done me a favor," she said. Then a smile covered her face. She took a couple of steps away and threw him the roll book.

"Here, you take roll." Then she laughed at the surprised look on his face.

"Where are you going?" he asked, sounding like any parent.

"I've got some errands to run. I think I'll take the day off."

"You want company?" Tom asked with a grin.

"I've got to do these myself," she said. "We'll have to play hookey together some other day."

"I'll count on it," he said. "Don't get in trouble now," his voice sounded with a sarcastic warning.

"I think it's about time I did." Bobbie called back from down the hall. "It might just take some of the pressure off you around here."

With that, they waved and Tom went back to class. Bobbie, on the other hand, went to the dean's office, not really looking for the dean as much as for Ryan. Sure enough, he was there, spending the last day of an in-school suspension.

"Ryan, we need to go to that intervention," she said.

"I've been sitting here thinking the same thing, but how?" he asked.

Ryan was sitting in the dean's outer office. The dean had his door closed. Bobbie knocked on the door.

"Don't bother. He walked out a few minutes ago," Ryan said.

Bobbie opened the door and found the dean's sport coat hanging on the coat tree. She reached in his pocket and found his car keys.

"Let's go," she said. Ryan looked as if he'd witnessed a miracle.

"We can explain later," Bobbie said. "There's no time now."

They walked back out into the hall. Ryan would not have gotten twenty feet without being stopped by a hall monitor, but with Bobbie next to him they got to the door by the teacher's parking lot before anyone stopped them.

"Where are you going?" the monitor asked. Ryan looked nervous but Bobbie quickly answered.

"We have a family emergency. The dean said we could use his car." With that, she turned and walked out and Ryan followed.

They knew which car was the dean's. All the students looked at it and drooled. It was a red sports car. When they got in and Bobbie started it and backed out, Ryan spoke with a new sense of respect.

"Welcome to the dark side, young Skywalker," Ryan said in a low voice making the Vader sound through his nose.

Bobbie drove quickly but safely to the treatment center.

CHAPTER 19

AT THE TREATMENT CENTER PAUL had finished speaking. It had gone smoothly. Molly could tell that Hank had been moved, but not convinced.

When Paul had said, ". . . and I'd like you to get help," Hank had said, "Well that depends. What kind of help are we talking about?"

"We want you to go to an outpatient treatment program here," Molly said. "You could keep on working and come here for treatment in the evening and then go to AA meetings on the weekend."

"Why can't I just quit drinking if that's the problem?" Hank asked belligerently.

"Perhaps I can help with that one," Jack said. "First of all, most people need help and support to quit. Molly has talked about numerous times you have said you'd quit or cut down and you haven't. I believe that's because you can't quit without help. More importantly, your drinking has affected you and your family not only physically, but also emotionally and spiritually. If you only quit drinking it just takes care of the physical problems. You all need help in those other areas of your lives."

"I don't know," said Hank. "Why aren't the rest of the family here?"

Molly had given a lot of thought to that question before he ever asked it. It was one she had anticipated. She knew very well that he would think, because of his denial, that the other children didn't think he had a problem. In spite of her fear about the conclusions he would draw, she decided that she didn't want to further the lack of direct communication in the family by speaking for Scott, Bobbie and Ryan. She had interpreted his behavior to them and theirs to him long enough.

"You'll have to ask them that yourself," she said.

Molly thought about how she needed to tell Hank about what would happen if he didn't stop drinking. Molly still wasn't sure what to say. She didn't want a divorce, but she was just beginning to see how the whole family was being affected by Hank's drinking and she couldn't continue to subject the children to that. She would start with the things she knew she would do and hope that Hank didn't see them as a threat.

She knew too that Jack would follow through on reporting him to child welfare.

The door opened and Molly knew these horrible possibilities would not be necessary yet.

"Now, Hank," she said, with tears of joy in her eyes, "you *can* ask them yourself."

Even though Jack had made it clear that anyone who had not participated in the final role-playing should not come to the intervention, he silently widened the circle. Bobbie and Ryan pulled up two extra chairs directly across from Hank.

"Why weren't you here for the rest of this?" Hank asked bluntly.

Ryan spoke first. His voice was different now. It was quiet and soft. He ignored his father's question and began with his own data.

"Dad, I remember a time recently when I had come home after drinking. I was throwing up in the bathroom and Bobbie and Mom were taking care of me. You came in after the noise woke you up from sleeping. You had been at the bar most of the afternoon and had missed dinner, so I guess you had drank a lot. When you saw I was sick and staggering you accused me of being drunk. I said, 'It takes one to know one.' You took my head and pushed it in the toilet. I couldn't breathe and I was scared.

"Mom made you let me up, and when I came up with my face filled with vomit I felt humiliated. Mom told you we'd talk about it in the morning, but the next day you didn't remember. I was relieved, but I was angry too, like a page had been torn out of my life that would never be finished."

Hank was quiet for a moment while he tried to make sense of what he heard.

"Yes, and it's stunts like that that get you in trouble all the time," Hank finally said. "Maybe we should be here talking about *your* drinking problem."

Ryan had a tear in his eye and his mouth went tight. Bobbie reached over and put her hand on his shoulder.

"Maybe you're right, Dad, but we're here to talk about you now," Ryan said. His voice was still soft. Molly was proud of how he controlled himself. In the past, he had always been hooked into fighting with Hank, but this time he hadn't.

"What, no smart ass comment?" Hank asked.

"No, Dad, I love you and I want you to get help."

Ryan said. Hank stared off in silence.

"Dad," Bobbie said. She was already crying, and had to stop until the lump left her throat.

"I'm here because I love you, but also because I love all of us. I didn't want to come here today because it was too hard for me to watch you go through this. You've always been my Dad, and even when you were drinking and making comments to me that embarrassed me, I loved you and respected you.

"But Daddy, I'm learning that we're all being hurt by your drinking. All my life I've been taking care of other people.

You were drinking and Mom was concerned with your drinking and that often left me to care for the smaller kids. No one told me I had to, but I did it just to keep peace. But Daddy, I'm missing growing up. I've spent my life already being a grownup. I want to be young and have fun like other kids. I want Paul to have friends and Ryan to show his good side. I want Scott to be human instead of perfect and I want Sally to be less confused.

"Please, Daddy, get help so we can all get better."

At the start of the intervention Hank had reminded Molly of the Wisconsin winters. He had been cold and frozen. When his brother talked he became like a mild day in January. He was pleasant enough but there was no hint of a thaw. Through each person's talk she saw a warming trend but still could only hope for springtime. When Ryan spoke so softly she knew spring was coming and with Bobbie it was confirmed when the ice in Hank melted and ran down his checks.

When he nodded his head "yes" he was sobbing like the stores of past frozen winters had broken loose. When the family gathered around him and touched him, it truly felt like summer.

"What do you want me to do?" he asked his family when he had stopped crying.

"We would like you to go now and get admitted into the outpatient program," Ken told him. "You could be finished by noon and even come to work if you wanted. Though you're more than welcome to the day off."

"With or without pay?" Hank quipped lamely.

Ken smiled. "With," he said, "but you'll have to take a vacation day."

Then for the first time either could remember, the two brothers hugged.

Jack took Hank to be admitted to the program. The family stood in a circle, holding hands. Molly looked up to heaven. "Thank God," she said simply. It was more than an expression.

Ken took Sally and Paul back to their school. Waiting for Hank, Molly sat smiling at Ryan and Bobbie. When she was about to thank them, they blurted out together, "Mom, we have a confession to make."

They told her the whole story. She tried for a while to look stern, but she was just too happy and relieved.

Besides, she kind of liked the idea of Bobbie breaking a few rules for a change.

Molly called the dean, who was understandably upset but also relieved to find his car was safe. Bobbie got her first detention ever, but the dean agreed not to press charges against them. The idea of the detention didn't bother Bobbie much, since she knew Tom would undoubtedly be there with her.

Molly thought it was time that she checked out the rumors that had floated around since grade school about the two of them.

CHAPTER 20

MOLLY SPENT THE REST OF the morning with Hank, getting him set in the outpatient treatment program. After they were finished, they took themselves out to lunch. They talked about the program they would be going through as a family. Hank admitted being scared and still somewhat in shock. He said he wanted to return to work and do something familiar for a while.

Molly's first thought was, "What happens after work?" But she didn't want to mention it and was glad when Hank said it would seem strange not stopping afterwards for a beer.

"I guess I'll be home early," he joked.

Molly decided to take the rest of the day off and go to see Josh at the hospital and tell him the good news.

She slipped up the same back stairway, then down the same corridor. As she turned the corner she saw the same nurse standing in front of his room. She thought to herself that after what she had been through this lady was no match for her. Approaching the nurse, Molly thought that the woman didn't even look as mean as she did before. As a matter of fact, she looked almost sad. What was happening hit Molly as she walked even closer and saw the tears in the nurse's eyes.

Molly began to shake her head and run toward the room, trying to bypass the nurse. But the nurse grabbed her around the waist.

"There's no one in there," the nurse said. "He died this morning."

Molly stopped struggling and the nurse turned her gently and held her.

"No," Molly cried. "God wouldn't do this to us. We deserve this one day to share together. Josh made this day for me. He has the right to know about it. After all the work and planning and tension I deserve one day just to enjoy it."

"I'm sorry," the nurse said. "He died peacefully this morning. There was no sign of pain or struggle."

Josh had told them less than a month ago that he was dying. Perhaps others were prepared for this, but to Molly it was a complete shock. She had been so busy with the intervention that she had no time for grieving. The last time she saw the doctor he had looked very ill, but he had been alert and talkative.

The memory of the last visit suddenly came flooding back to her. How she had been hurried out of the room after he had talked about his fear of losing her friendship. How she had never been able to respond. She pushed herself away from the nurse.

"How important do your damn visiting hours seem to you now?" Molly yelled. "The last time I saw him you had to make sure I wasn't there more than fifteen minutes."

"I'm sorry," the nurse replied gently.

"You're full of those today, after it's too late, aren't you?" Molly said with fury in her voice. Then she was instantly sorry for her outrage.

"I guess I'm the one who should apologize," Molly said to the nurse. "I just can't believe he's gone." She began to cry.

She cried for the loss of their relationship and the things she never had a chance to say; for the things she didn't know she felt and the thoughts she still had to sort out in her mind.

Suddenly, Molly felt exhausted. This was just too much for one day. She left the hospital and drove home slowly, just barely able to keep her eyes open enough to see the road. When she arrived at home she went to the couch and fell asleep. She woke up when Paul and Sally came home from school. They had heard about Josh's death from their teachers in their classes. He had been a friend to the whole family, so they, too, were sad.

"Will we still go to treatment?" Paul wondered out loud. A new wave of sadness touched Molly. What if this put a damper on the whole process? It would be hard enough getting help for Hank's alcoholism, much less dealing with the loss they all felt with Josh. Finally Paul's question filtered its way through her mind. She looked as if she just had a jolt.

"Oh! Yes, Paul. We can't wait with that," she said. "Josh would want us to continue, I know."

He would, she thought. She knew she couldn't postpone this now, or Hank might never get help.

When Bobbie and Ryan got home from school, she shared the news with them too. Bobbie went to her room and cried. Ryan simply sat and stared. Hank came home early as he had said he would, only to find the place like a morgue. He held Molly after she told him and she was surprised at his compassion.

"We don't have to go tonight, if you'd rather wait," he offered.

"No," she said firmly. "I think it's important that we start right now. It may even help us through this."

So they started treatment that night. They attended lectures and took part in a family therapy session. They also split off for individual and group meetings. The second night, they also visited the funeral parlor where Josh was being waked. Hank, however, stayed at the center.

The counselor said he was beginning to have withdrawal symptoms from the alcohol. Hank swore it was the flu, but he agreed to stay anyway, which was a change in itself. A t the wake, Molly looked at Josh and spoke with several of her friends, colleagues and acquaintances, but it all seemed unreal to her. The man she saw in the casket was not Josh. And, though she spoke about him to others, it seemed to her he would soon walk over and join the conversation as he always had at community functions.

CHAPTER **21**

THE FUNERAL WAS SATURDAY. HANK left the treatment center, although he was still pretty sick, and even Scott came home from college. Molly sat at the organ and looked at her family all lined up in the pew. It was the first time Hank had been in church in years and since the older kids had grown up they hadn't gone very often either. So this was perhaps the very first time they had all been there together in a long time.

She could tell even by the way they sat that something had changed. Scott sat on the end of the pew, a little apart from everyone else. Paul sat next to him and then Sally. Bobbie sat next to Sally and Ryan sat next to her.

At the other end of the pew, close to Ryan, was Hank.

She wondered what would happen to each of them.

Scott seemed distant from the family and even from his father. He looked depressed and his nose was running, though he didn't seem to have any other symptoms of a cold. Perhaps Molly was too suspicious, but she wondered about the cocaine epidemic that had supposedly hit the country and especially college campuses. It seemed particularly popular among intellectuals and athletes, and Scott fit into both categories.

She cringed at the thought of doing another intervention and she wondered if family ties would ever be that important to Scott.

Paul had seemed to make the biggest change so far.

He had already brought a friend home after school.

Sally seemed more confused than ever, but that was understandable with so many things happening so quickly.

Bobbie had announced she had a date for Saturday night.

Molly had consented, though she didn't like the boy. She wondered if Bobbie had traded taking care of Sally and Paul for taking care of Tom. But it was just a date, and Molly tried not to make a big deal of it. Ryan seemed the same in some respects, but he did seem to be getting along much better with Hank.

As for Hank, he had expressed resentment at the way they had gotten him into treatment. But he did admit he couldn't think of what else might have done it. He had also told Molly in the privacy of their bedroom that he was going through treatment for his family's sake and still was not convinced he was an alcoholic, as the counselors seemed to be trying to tell him.

He said he thought he still might be able to drink socially. That scared Molly, but she was learning, too, to take life one day at a time. He wasn't drinking now and he still had a month of treatment and AA meetings to go through. If he pretended long enough, and listened, maybe some things would rub off. She knew now that the family would handle it differently if he did drink again.

She also thought that she herself had changed, but she was a little vague as to how. It's always hardest to see yourself, she thought.

A cough startled her from her thoughts and she was surprised to see how the church had filled from the time her family had entered. She looked down at her watch and was startled to see that Pastor Brooks was waiting to start the service. She announced the entrance hymn and began to play.

Molly thought Pastor Brooks looked tired and sad as he proceeded through the service. She wondered if he had had the time to prepare a eulogy. She thought the worried look on his face indicated that he hadn't. At the eulogy, the priest paused for a moment and then began to speak in a rather apologetic voice.

"As I hope all of you can appreciate, I've been very busy over the last couple of days and haven't had much time to prepare words for this morning. I hope all of you know how much I loved this man and think that he deserves the very best. I won't use time as an excuse, however, because it was from a commitment to him that I didn't prepare anything. Instead I'll read a letter he had prepared and asked me to read." Pastor Brooks reached for a letter he had placed on the podium before the service.

"I've read this letter several times, hoping I could get through it without crying. I've yet to make it, so I doubt I'll do it this time." He cleared his throat, hoping it would cover up the fact that he had already started to cry:

My dear friends,

You probably thought you had heard the last of me, but here I am again speaking to you.

As I'm sure you have gathered by now, I wrote this before I died. You may think I'm going to tell you not to mourn, but I'm not. I spent too much of my life trying to talk people out of feelings, so I won't do it now. I loved you people and I think you loved me back, so it's only fitting that you grieve. It's good and healthy to grieve the loss of a loved one. I just don't want you grieving for the wrong reasons. So I'm trying to anticipate what you may be thinking as you cry.

Some of you may think I died too early, and there is a part of me that certainly agrees with that.

Had I gone with the averages, I might have lived fifteen more years. But I learned something too late in my life, and that is that sometimes it takes a crisis to make me move. Without the knowledge that I was dying, I would not have had the courage to ask you to sing, and you might not have been willing to sing. Now let me tell you this: I would not give up that Sunday when you sang my songs for anything—even 15 more years of the status quo.

I have been thinking about the words of that first song I asked you to sing: "Be not afraid; I go before you always. Come follow me."

I'd like you to follow me—not in dying, but in risking. I can't promise that all of your risks will pay off, but it beats living a life of fear or stagnation.

After that Sunday, I took some risks that didn't work, but I don't regret any of them. Sometimes I felt happy, sometimes sad, but always alive. You all risked singing the songs I wanted you to sing. Now I have one more request. Sing your own songs. Take the risk of living a creative life. Don't live a life praying for miracles. Go out and make one—or perhaps a dozen.

I am now on a new adventure that I'm excited about. As a Christian, I spent a lifetime preparing for this moment, so I don't want to run from it. I don't know if I'm allowed to keep an eye on you from where I'll be, but it would not fit my conception of heaven without that ability. I have spent the sixty plus years of my life involved in your lives. It is inconceivable to me that this would stop abruptly . . . or ever, for that matter.

My conception of heaven would be that I'd be a mother eagle teaching you all to fly. Perhaps that's why I like that song "On Eagles' Wings" so much. I would fly each of you to the heavens, then drop you to earth.

You would have to risk flying to save yourselves. With any luck you'd take off and fly on your own. But, if not, I'd swoop down and catch you on my back and take you safely back to the heavens. But soon I'd drop you again, till you could experience free flight. When you took your first solo I'd cry from the heavens and glory in your accomplishments. I also hope some day to be reunited with all of you.

But for now this is good-bye. And I love you.

Forever, Dr. Joshua Krueger

P.S. If you could find it in your heart to sing "Be Not Afraid" one more time I'll do my best to listen wherever I may be.

P.P.S. I wouldn't mind "On Eagles' Wings" at the end, either.

About halfway through the letter, the pastor gave up trying to stop crying and let the tears flow. After the sermon he said, "I really don't know what I can add to that. Certainly that letter speaks to the man that he was. You can bet at the proper moment I'll be singing

'Be Not Afraid.' I hope you'll join me."

When the time came, Molly announced the song and the people tried singing. It was not as loud as that first Sunday with Josh, even though the church was more full.

It wasn't that the people didn't try. They did. It was just hard to sing through the tears. People's mouths would open but a sob rather than a song would emerge.

They sang "On Eagles' Wings" on the way out of church. Perhaps walking helped, but for whatever reason, they sang louder.

CHAPTER 22

THE FAMILY HAD FINISHED TREATMENT and school was out for the summer before Molly was ready to visit Josh's grave. She went at a time, in the heat of the day, when she was sure of being alone. She had the windows down in the car. This summer, for some reason, she didn't use her air conditioning. Nothing felt better to her than allowing the sights, sounds, and smells of summer to wash over her. A car passed her with a dog sticking his head out the window, and she wished she could do the same. She wished, too, that she could walk and talk with her friend rather than standing over his grave. She missed talking to him and telling him about each of the members of the family and what he or she was doing.

So when she stopped to visit his grave she chatted with him much the way she would have if he'd been alive:

"I'm so sorry, old friend. It's been so long without my visiting you. I guess it's hard for me to do two things at once. I've been so busy with my family since the intervention, I just haven't had time. Nor, I guess, did I have the courage to face my feelings for you.

"You sure were right about so many things. First, about risk. It was scary to do that intervention!

And there has been pain and sadness as well as joy as a result of it. But it certainly did produce change. Scott still seems distant from the family and I'm more convinced than ever he has problems with drugs. But Hank and I have been talking openly about it. Hank is less convinced than I am, but he did say the other night we should confront Scott with our concerns.

"Bobbie is still dating Tom. He's less of a jerk than I thought, but I still hope she doesn't settle on anyone for a long time. I wish she could just have fun for a while, and not be so darned serious. Ryan is still angry and fights a lot, but both he and Bobbie are attending Alateen and also a new group called Adult Children of Alcoholics that seems to be helping them. It is the older children that seem more 'stuck' in their patterns.

"Paul and Sally seem more flexible and more trusting of the changes. Paul has two boys now that he pals around with. He seems to like it best when they call him, but he enjoys their company enough that, if he doesn't see them for a while, he calls them. Sally is still a clown, but she seems willing to live with tension a little more rather than making a joke to relieve it. She also seems to have her feet on the ground more and is not running in a million different directions like she use to be.

"As for me, you were right there, too. Hank wants more of my time now. Sometimes I enjoy it, but at others, I'd rather be with my music. He also wants to be more involved with the children and I feel a little jealous about the place that he's taking in their hearts and lives. Yet my worst fear is that he'll drink again. Each night, even if he's five minutes late, I picture him in the bar. I realize more and more that I was as involved in alcohol as he was, and in many ways I think it'll take me longer to recover.

I'm still afraid of my feelings. I still go to Al-Anon meetings, but it still seems as though other people's lives are so different from mine. I know that's denial, but it seems so hard to break through.

"But enough about my family, dear friend. It's time that you and I talk. You and I talk! Listen to me. You can't talk. I don't even know if you can listen. But you taught me to hope again, and I can hope that you can hear this. I also hope you can understand it, because I don't know if I do.

"The worst part of where I was is that I didn't know my own feelings. I'm angry at you for not trusting more in our friendship and not being more willing to risk that sooner than you did. Believe it or not, I'm not sad for me that it didn't happen sooner. I'm not even sure it would have worked sooner. But I am sad for you, because I wish you could have been a part of it. As the family doctor you could have added a lot, and I sure could have used your support.

"I just wish you could have at least the pleasure of hearing me say 'thank you' for teaching me to risk again, and for pushing me to do the intervention. Because, in spite of the pain, I think the whole family and I are healthier for it. Even if Hank should go back to drinking, I know we would cope with it differently.

"But the anger was just the first feeling. It didn't take me long to forgive you, dear friend. After all, even doctors have a right to be human. Besides, when I thought about it more, I felt guilty. I realized you may not have trusted in our friendship because I never let you know how I felt about you. Even worse, I never let myself know how I felt. I'm beginning to realize that I may have grown up in an alcoholic family myself. I didn't want my children to grow up in a family without talk, trust, or feeling the way I now realize that my brothers and sister and I did, but that's exactly what was happening before you pushed me to do something about it. I couldn't let you know about my feelings because I couldn't face them myself.

"So, dear friend, don't feel guilty for eternity that you didn't confront me soon enough. I should be thanking you for letting me experience closeness in a friendship, even if I did realize too late how important it was to me. Maybe I can have that closeness with others now, thanks to you. But I'll wish forever that I could have told you before you died and that I would have had at least a short time to experience it with you."

For the first time since Josh's death, Molly really let all her feelings go. She knelt down by his grave and pounded the ground. "Why did you have to die without knowing how I felt about you?" she sobbed.

Suddenly she heard a cry in the sky. She looked high above her and an eagle soared. The bird cried again. Molly never saw coincidence in the same way again.

CHAPTER 1: A NOVEL IDEA

For as long as there has been school, which in some of our cases dates back almost to the one room schoolhouse, the textbook has been king. Once we moved past Dick and Jane, teachers used textbooks in all subjects except reading and literature for in-school and homework assignments. There is good reason for this: textbooks provide information. In the counseling profession textbooks can teach things like symptoms, diagnosis, and treatment. Though not advocating the elimination of textbooks, novels and stories, even poetry, are often overlooked as supplemental reading. There are several reasons why stories are not only a valuable part of counselor education but worthwhile for clients as well.

Though today's brain research has gone far beyond the simple left and right models of earlier days, the left and right brain can still be used as a metaphor for more complex models and serves our purposes here. Whatever the case, different functions take place in different parts of the brain. Things like logic, spelling, grammar, time and math, are handled by one part of the brain - once referred to as left brain thinking and space; relationships, pictures, music, and creativity take place in a different part - referred to as right brain thinking. Things like feelings are processed in still another part of the brain - sometimes referred to as our animal brain.

It takes different stimuli to access different parts. Textbooks tend to appeal to the left brain and are an essential source of information. However, counselors must be able to utilize other sources of information as well as clients also need to access other parts of their brains to heal. Things like pictures and novels stimulate the part of the brain that is interested in relationships, feelings and creativity. Counselors and clients must be able to deal with feelings, spirituality, sexuality, and social issues.

Stories tap into the unconscious parts of our human psyche. No one demonstrated this more successfully than Milton Erickson. In his younger days Erickson used a powerful voice and a keen sense of nonverbal perception to create trance and change. However, as he aged and his voice and his legs were affected by the ravages of polio he had as a child, he began to use stories to create the same effect.

Stories can be powerful motivators as well. Can you remember a textbook that motivated you to make a change in your life? How about a story? It doesn't matter whether the story is real or fiction, reading about someone overcoming an obstacle often challenges one to take on obstacles standing in his/her way.

Another reason why stories can be a valuable education tool is they can cover the beginning, the middle and end of a problem. Textbooks will often use a case study to make a point, often giving us just a segment of a counseling session that fits with a point the author wishes to make. It may leave one to wonder how did the problem develop, what was the motivating moment that made the client decide they couldn't do it alone? Besides counseling, what were other factors in their life that brought them along on the road to recovery?

Another factor that can be shown in stories is the courage it takes for clients to begin counseling. Many years ago Carl Rogers talked about respect as one of the core conditions in counseling. Nothing encourages a counselor to respect a client more than when he sees the courage it takes for the client to initiate counseling and show the vulnerability it takes to get better.

While sitting through a lecture, a sermon, or other presentation notice how the room changes when the speaker tells a story - especially if it is a good one. Coughing and fidgeting will stop, the room will grow quiet; and there will be an attentiveness that wasn't there previously. Perhaps it is a reminder of the stories we enjoyed that were told to us as children at bedtime.

Another lesson we learned from Erickson is that stories do not always have an immediate impact. One of the original storytellers was Jesus. Notice how often in His stories he talked about planting seeds. This not only activates the unconscious, it is also a metaphor of how stories often work. Stories plant seeds that sometimes take a long time to germinate. This also gives the counselor hope. Sometimes clients leave a counselor's office with no visible or auditory indication of change, but if a story has been told, a "seed" may start to grow long after the client leaves.

A story maintains interest. This is not always so with a textbook. For example, a student sits down with a text book, perhaps studying for a test. Despite the motivation to do well, often by the time the bottom of the page is reached, he or she can't remember a word of the text. The process is repeated but the result is the same. Now think about the last story you read. Maybe you sat down to read a page or two, or maybe you were just going to read until you got tired before bed. Next thing you know it is well after you had planned to be asleep but you couldn't put the book down.

Another advantage to stories is they put you in the middle of the action. Too often texts are just words; stories are sights and sounds, emotion, sensations, smells and tastes. The reader is often are a participant, feeling what the character feels instead of being just an observer. In counseling we call this empathy. Stories touch the soul.

Appreciate the saying "God created people because of His love of stories". Thomas Moore, author of Care of the Soul, was reluctant to define the soul other than to say it is beyond definition and is what we have not discovered yet. But the soul has a place in counseling, maybe it is part of our spirituality, but we should refrain from the religious definition of the soul. To use a title from a book by Canfield and Hansen, stories are Chicken Soup for the Soul.

Assignments can be more meaningful when based on stories. A teacher or counselor may ask the client or student what he or she would do in a situation from a story; they may even suggest the student or client write their own story or change the ending.

Finally, stories are a must in some cultures. One of the reasons we are so drawn to the American Indian is the importance of stories in their culture. Counselors wanting to work with the American Indian population better become a storyteller.

CHAPTER 2: INTERVENTION

Intervention is a way for friends, family, coworkers, and employers to get help for someone they care about that is having a problem. An intervention is often used if that problem is substance abuse or addiction, but it can be used for any issue where denial or a lack of motivation to get help is involved. People in the Addictions field will often say that addiction is the only disease where the person afflicted refuses to admit to the existence of the disease, however, that can be true of any illness or disorder.

How often do adult children worry about their aging parents living alone and yet when they suggest getting help for that parent the parent refuses? Schizophrenics often refuse to take their medication either because they don't like the way it makes them feel, or because they don't want to admit they are sick. Bipolar patients often don't want to take their medicine because they miss their manic phases. Sometimes people who are out of work don't want to begin searching for a new job because they are afraid of rejection, still grieving the loss of their old job, too afraid to try retraining, or are just enjoying the freedom of not working. Some people don't believe smoking is an addiction or that it affects other people. These are just a few instances where there is denial or a lack of motivation and perhaps intervention can help.

So what is intervention and how does it work? Quite simply it is presenting the afflicted person with the reality of their situation in a loving, non-judgmental way. There are a number of different opinions about how to proceed with an intervention; some are based on the setting in which a professional works. It is often suggested that typical interventions cover at least four sessions over a three-week period. However, a former student who worked on a crisis line in Iowa reported teaching people to do interventions in ten minutes. Let's proceed with the idea that there are at least four parts to an intervention and the more thoroughly each part is covered the more likely the intervention will be successful. However, the term "successful" is used with trepidation.

What constitutes success? Is it that the afflicted person goes through an assessment, goes into treatment, the involved participants learn healthier ways to communicate, the behavior in question becomes less enjoyable and more likely to be dropped later, and all involved leave better off in some way? The answer to all of those questions is yes.

The first goal of an intervention should be to get the targeted person to an assessment not treatment. It is the job of the person doing the assessment to determine the need and also the level of treatment required. Second, not all interventions are successful right away. In the case of the Brandt family from Sober Spring, Hank was willing to go into treatment right away but Scott was not. It can be assumed however that the intervention played an important part in his eventual treatment. It may happen that the targeted person never gets help but family, friends and coworkers develop more effective coping mechanisms to deal with the problem. We will cover more variations and opinions as we go along but for now let's get started on what needs to be addressed in an intervention.

Stage1:

An intervention will usually start because someone is in pain due to the actions of a person close to him/her. This might vary from a substance they are using, to a process they are addicted to, a behavior, etc. For example, in Sober Spring, Molly is concerned with heavy alcohol use of a partner.

The first things that need to happen are an assessment and education. It is important to find out if the problem being reported is indeed the problem. In nearly every case it is, but there are exceptions. In the case of addictions, cases have been reported where a teenager is out of control; the parents come in because they are hoping to get to the root of the problem, yet as they are interviewed there is almost no evidence of alcohol or drug use. Other cases that have occurred are of spouses reporting that their partners are acting strangely, perhaps from an addiction of some sort, but upon assessment it seems more likely their partners are having an affair. The assessment is also important because if the complaining parties cannot convince the counselor of a problem they will never have enough data to break through the denial of someone addicted to drugs or alcohol. It is not uncommon for a counselor to be convinced there is a problem but there is not nearly enough data to proceed with an intervention. This is why a counselor doing an intervention must be well trained in alcoholism and addiction, gerontology or any other area where an intervention may be required. Doing an intervention with co-therapists can double the chances of having needed expertise. (For knowledge in addiction and other problems the reader can begin with other chapters in this book.)

Education can be important for the opposite reason. The person coming in is in pain and has plenty of data but believes all alcoholics are skid row bums. They just want their partner to cut back a little or do their drinking at home. It is also important at this point to suggest that all involved in the intervention, especially family members, get help (see the chapter on family dynamics of addiction). Information on such self help groups as Alanon, Alateen, Families Anonymous etc. should be available, including where and when a meetings is scheduled.

The next goal should be to introduce the concept of writing the alcoholic a letter.

To do this the counselor must be familiar with confrontation skills. Every person alive who has the language skills to communicate should learn confrontation skills.

The first hurdle for the counselor is convincing those involved that they need to write a letter rather than just tell the alcoholic what they are feeling. Practicing what they are preaching, the counselor might want to include the following reasons in writing.

1. When the actual intervention takes place there will be a great deal of tension. For anyone who has ever given a speech or been in a play, no matter how well lines have been memorized, when you are faced with an audience those lines are easy to forget. Now triple the amount of tension - confronting a loved

one with a subject that everyone avoids because they are afraid to talk about it, even to each other, is extremely difficult.

2. Writing helps to organize thoughts. By the time things have gotten bad enough for an intervention to take place family, friends and coworkers may have dealt with the problem for years. Deciding on which incidents should be mentioned and how to describe them is easier to put down on paper or a computer screen.

3. Writing breaks through the family denial. As mentioned earlier, often one or more members of the group may want to minimize the severity of the problem; however, after seeing their own experiences with the alcoholic they are convinced the problem is real and serious.

4. Reading what you have written helps avoid eye contact. Having taught interpersonal skills for years this concept is foreign to me, but it is best in an intervention to avoid eye contact. Over the years an addict has learned defense mechanisms. One of the ways is non-verbally using eye contact to intimidate, or get sympathy, or countless other manipulations. So, as we learned in grade school, it is best to keep your eyes on your own paper.

5. Avoid interruptions. In normal conversations we are used to interrupting one another, particularly if we have an objection. When we are reading something prepared the listener is more likely to let us finish.

6. A written statement can be corrected. Even the best of us, well trained in confrontation, often revert to street fighting tactics in important and painful situations. As you will see in stage two of the intervention process the counselor will review and correct the letters. Once completed the counselor can be more confident in what will transpire once the actual intervention takes place.

7. Letters can be corrected from a distance. People will often participate in an intervention from all over the country as those from out of town can't be expected to fly in once a week. With

the advent of e-mail it is easy to send letters back and forth with suggestions and corrections from the counselor.

How to write the letters: Do's and Don'ts

1. Avoid judgment. The objective is not to convince the alcoholic they are bad or sinful, in fact it is just the opposite. As stated earlier, it is not necessary to convince them they are an alcoholic, only that there is a problem and they need help.

2. We not only want to avoid sounding or looking judgmental, we also want to avoid judgmental terminology. For instance, when describing an event it may seem quick and easy to say, "You were drunk." It is better, however, to use what you gain through your senses. The model for confrontation is: I observe, I interpret, I feel. So rather than saying, "You were drunk", you might say, "I saw you stagger when you walked, I heard you slur your words, I could smell alcohol on your breath, I interpreted that to mean you were drinking, and I felt afraid because you were driving."

3. Never, never, never, ask questions. When we do an intervention we want the person to listen not talk. Asking a question invites them to take the floor and respond - that is the last thing we want. So don't say, "Do you remember?" Say, "I remember." Not, "How would you feel?", but, "I feel."

4. Do use observation, interpretation, and feeling. Especially when dealing with alcohol and drugs keep interpretation, which is like assumption, to a minimum because it gives the alcoholic something to argue about.

5. Use "I." Talk about incidents in which the drinking affected you and how. See the letters in Sober Spring, and Flight of the Loon, for specific examples.

Stage 2

Probably the most demanding stage of the intervention for the counselor is stage two. The counselor must review the letters, decide on the order in which they are read, and the seating arrangement. The counselor must help the group develop a plan, assign roles for getting information, and help the individuals decide on their bottom lines. Determine the date, location and time of the intervention. It must be decided how everyone will get to the intervention and how to get the alcoholic to attend. Some suggest deciding on a member of the group to present the plan. This stage can often take several hours, possibly several sessions.

Reviewing the letters

Once participants in the intervention have returned with their letters the counselor will ask them to read them out loud to the rest of the group. It is important for the counselor to tell each person they may be interrupted if changes need to be made, otherwise, important feedback may be forgotten. The counselor may also want to take notes as this is the time for determining the order of the letters. The rule is to start and end with the strongest letters and build as you go along to the end.

There are three factors in determining the strength of the letters. One is deciding who has the provided the best examples that point out there is a problem. In describing behavior all the senses can be involved. As mentioned earlier use phrases such as, "I heard you slur your words, saw you stagger when you walked, tasted alcohol in your soft drink, smelled alcohol on your breath, felt for a heartbeat when you had passed out." The second important factor is feeling. This includes both the verbal and non-verbal reporting of feeling. We tell people in the group not to hold back tears or fear; it is important to let the alcoholic know just how their drinking and alcoholic behavior has affected them. The only feelings we discourage are anger and resentment and this is because the alcoholic will use these to start an argument, possibly causing them to "storm out" and effectively end the intervention.

The third factor in determining the order of the letters is the relationship to the alcoholic and this sometimes can trump the first two. Even though the wife or husband of the alcoholic may have the best data and report and demonstrate the most emotion, at times it may be best to sandwich the spouse in the middle of the other participants because their relationship is often very strained at this point and their spouse has repeatedly heard what they have had to say. If there is a boss in the group they often have the most influential relationship with the alcoholic.

Relationship also has a factor in seating arrangements. By the time the alcoholic arrives everyone else should be present and seated. There should only be one chair open in which the alcoholic can sit and that should be between the most influential people in the room. These people have a special job. When the alcoholic walks into the room the counselor or group designated person stands and says, for example quoting from Sober Spring, "Hi Hank, my name is Jack. I believe you know the rest of these people. They are here today because they care about you and they are concerned about your drinking. They have prepared some things they want you to hear. Will you listen?"

At this point it is important to get a commitment that he will listen. Once he agrees and sits down the person designated to go first - usually one of the people next to the alcoholic - begins to read. If the alcoholic interrupts, the reader should avoid eye contact while the people on either side of him gently place their hand on his arm and say, "(client name), you said you'd listen." It is easiest and least confusing if the rest of the letters are read in order of the seating arrangements so that the last letter read is by the significant person on the other side of the alcoholic. Only two other people need be designated in the seating. The counselor should sit directly across from the alcoholic. Group dynamics research indicates that we are most likely to get angry with the person directly across from us. Since all the other people in the room will probably have a continuing relationship with the alcoholic the counselor has the least to lose if the alcoholic is angry with him. The second person may be someone who sits between the alcoholic and the door. This person's job is to stand up if the alcoholic threatens to leave and remind him that he agreed to listen. They should not in any way block the door, but it is one more voice of reason that may help the person agree to get help. Experience shows the person rarely threatens to leave, but family and friends almost always think this will happen. Anything to help assure them is beneficial.

Another crucial step in stage two is helping to develop a plan. If the person does agree to go through an assessment it is important that he go immediately. Therefore, an appointment for the assessment should be set up ahead of time. If, as is often the case, it is determined in the assessment that the person needs treatment and/or detox that also should be arranged in advance. Who will pay for the assessment and treatment? Does the person have insurance? If so, what is covered in the policy? If there is no insurance is there a public treatment center or perhaps counseling and AA meetings available? Sometimes churches or a friend or relative will fund treatment. Different people in the group should be assigned the task of getting this information before the next meeting. If the person works for a company where there is an Employee Assistance Program much of this information is readily available. The group will also want to discuss any excuses the person may give for not going to treatment right away and how they can counteract these excuses.

The first goal in an intervention is to get the person to address his problem because people care about him and are concerned about his situation, however, sometimes care and concern are not enough. When people read their letters each one should end with, "I want you to get help." After all the letters have been read the counselor, or group designee, presents the plan. If the person agrees he/she is taken immediately for an assessment. If they do not agree the group goes into their "bottom lines." There is a great deal of discrepancy among practitioners as to how to utilize the bottom line.

First of all what is the bottom line? All efforts should be utilized to keep the alcoholic from seeing it as a threat, but no matter how much effort the group makes to avoid it that is probably the way it will be perceived by someone with a toxic brain. One of the goals of an intervention is to stop the people who surround the alcoholic from enabling them. This is not only harmful for the alcoholic it is usually painful for the enabler. For instance, if a wife calls the boss after a weekend of heavy drinking and says, "My husband is sick," it not only makes it easier for the alcoholic, it also makes the wife feel guilty for being less than truthful. A potential bottom line for the wife is to say, "I will no longer tell your boss you are sick when you are hung-over." The question is when should she say this and how? My suggestion is to keep the bottom line separate from the letters. If the alcoholic agrees to enter treatment because people love and care about him and not because he feels threatened it can give him more time in treatment to work on his problem rather than working through his resentment.

There are those who believe it adds to the power of the letters to include the bottom line. Still another approach is for the support people to include themselves in the plan and to say to the alcoholic, "Here is what we are going to do to get better, will you join us?" Whatever the approach, it is important to work with the group on what they are willing to do to take care of themselves but *only* on those things they are committed to start tomorrow. We do not want a spouse to say, "If you don't get help I am filing for divorce" unless she is committed to taking him to an assessment and following through with the divorce if he doesn't agree to get help.

Another issue to be determined by the group is when and where the intervention is to take place. There are many factors that determine the time of the meeting. Obviously it needs to take place when most, if not all, of the group can be present. If there are people involved from out of town, select a time when can they arrange to be present. If getting everyone together is impossible perhaps someone is willing to read two letters - their own and that of whomever is unable to be present. Sometimes the absent person can videotape themselves reading their letter.

Work schedules need to be considered. In the best of all worlds it is recommended the intervention take place Tuesday through Thursday, shortly after the person wakes up. For the person who works during the day Monday through Friday 8:00 am might be a good time. For people who use substances and even process addictions, use is generally heaviest during the weekend. Therefore, Monday is not good a good day because the person may still be drunk or high on Monday morning; Friday is not good because often they will start to "party" on Thursday night. For people who work nights, swing shifts, weekends, are unemployed or work out of their homes we must rely on the knowledge of the group to determine the best time.

Perhaps the most complicated challenge for the group is where the intervention will take place and how to get the person there. If at all possible the intervention should take place in a professional office. People are usually on their best behavior in such a setting. Perhaps the next best setting is a meeting room at work (this is assuming of course that the work place is a willing participant and fully supportive of the intervention). It is our experience if the work place is involved and supportive, interventions have a high likelihood of success, but involving work can be risky. If the work place has no knowledge of the problem, or is not supportive of treatment they can find a variety of reasons for termination. If the company has an Employee Assistance Program chances are better that the company will be supportive. The next alternative is the home of a friend or relative, but it is not recommend to do an intervention in the person's home. This is their "castle" so to speak and we are intruders.

One example should suffice. A male and female counselor did an intervention together. After hours of considering where to do the intervention the group came to the conclusion that the only place it could possibly happen was the home. The co- counselors later recounted this story to a class they were teaching on intervention. The male remembered that the alcoholic had a gun collection and the wife met them at the door and said, "I THINK I got them all." The female remembered that she was relieved because the very overweight man came down the stairs to the group waiting in the family room wearing clothes because his wife said he often came down naked. In the future these two concluded they would not do an intervention in the alcoholic's home and if that was the only alternative they would prepare the group as much as possible but would not be present for the actual intervention. There may also be certain legal complications with doing an intervention in the alcoholic's home.

Another question is how to get the alcoholic to the intervention. This is another advantage if work is involved because a person can simply be asked to attend a meeting in a conference room. We have heard that some counselors suggest that a spouse or a designated person propose an outing for ice cream or a drink and then stop at the place designated for the intervention and say, "I just have to stop here for a minute. Come on in with me, I want to show you something."

We recommend being as honest as possible without giving away the actual intervention. In the case of a spouse, such as Molly, she can tell her partner she is going for counseling at XYZ treatment center and even ask him to come along. He will probably refuse as Hank did. But once the intervention has been established she can say, "The counselor asked that you just come once to tell your side." This often works and the honesty, like saving the bottom lines, will decrease the amount of time working through resentment during treatment.

Finally, it is important that everyone is clear on the time and that everyone arrive at least 15 minutes early. If there are children involved make sure they have a ride to the intervention. Two things need to be noted here:

1. Once the intervention starts the door is usually locked and no one is allowed to enter. In Sober Spring when Bobby and Ryan entered late this was done to add to the excitement of the story and usually would not be allowed. However, if it is apparent that an intervention is not going well and two significant people arrive that might make a difference, opening the door for them may be something the counselor would want to consider.

2. There is disagreement in the field about the age at which a young person might be allowed in an intervention. Some people have a hard and fast rule, which is no one younger than eight years old should be allowed to participate. There are good reasons for this, one reason is young children are easily manipulated. Another is they maybe too young to read and therefore we are not sure what they will say. Most importantly, they are vulnerable to later reprisals if the intervention doesn't go well. All

these need to be considered, but on the other hand if a child simply says with tears in their eyes, "Daddy please get help," no letter, no matter how heartfelt and eloquent can be more powerful.

Stage Three

The third stage of the intervention is practice. It is usually done the night before the actual intervention. There are a number of reasons for this timing. One, it is helpful for people coming from long distances. They need only find lodging for one night. Second, practicing in close proximity to the actual intervention decreases the chance of forgetting things such as seating arrangements, order of the letters being read, the time the intervention starts, etc.

Usually the counselor will play the part of the alcoholic, but a role player can be brought in as well. It is a good idea for whoever plays the part to do some of the things that the family is afraid will happen such as interruptions, threats to leave, and not agreeing to get help. After the session is finished the counselor may want to once again remind everyone about the time and make sure everyone has a ride to the intervention.

It should be noted that particularly for your first several interventions sleep might be hard to come by on this night between rehearsal and the intervention. Depending on the health of the family you may be wondering whether they will be on time, will they stick to their letters; will the alcoholic goad them into an argument? Will he agree to an assessment? We recommend this is a good time to practice several of the guidelines of AA. *One step at a time, first things first, let go and let God,* just to name a few.

If all goes well the intervention will be your shortest meeting. Even if the alcoholic doesn't agree to go right away, interventions usually don't last an hour. Some people like to plan a celebration afterward such as lunch. If it doesn't go well there is hope that it will have an impact in time. At the very least, everyone including the counselor can feel good that they have done what they can to help save a life.

There are those who do not believe in interventions, that the only real chance for an alcoholic to turn their life around is suffering the consequences of their drinking. The best argument we have heard against this is sixty percent of alcoholics die of the disease - to counselors that is too serious a consequence.

Classroom activities:

1. Confronting someone about his/her behavior need not be about alcohol or drugs, it might simply be something they did, or did not do, said or did not say, that left you with uncomfortable feelings. The important thing is to use all of the tools of writing a letter: *I observe* ..... *I interpret that to mean* and *I felt*. At the next class read them aloud. It is important for every one to practice listening for statements that are judgmental, use of right and wrong, bad and good, analytical statements, overuse of anger and/or resentment. Practice other ways to make the same points that are clearer, more concrete, more compassionate, etc.

2. Choose someone in the class to be "it". Give this person a particular problem from which you can do an intervention. Since you are only looking for an opportunity to practice the skills and not make someone uncomfortable, choose someone who is not going to be hurt by the process or the problem given. Pick the youngest person in the class to be an aging parent that needs help in maintaining their home, for example. The homework assignment is for everyone except the person who is "it" to choose a relationship to that person (son, daughter, friend, coworker, etc.) and to write a letter from that perspective. During the next class go through stages two, three and four.

Review the letters, make corrections, decide on seating arrangements, and based on the quality of the letters and the relationships determine the order of reading the letters. Depending on time constraints you may want to develop a plan as well as the other tasks for stage two. Then do the rehearsal and the intervention. Even though these are serious issues you don't have to be afraid to have some fun as long as no one gets hurt and the issues are given the respect they deserve.

References

I'll Quit Tomorrow: A Practical Guide to Alcoholism Treatment
By Vernon E. Johnson www.barnesandnoble.com 1990

Vernon Johnson—Wikipedia, the free encyclopedia
https://en.wikipedia.org/wiki/Vernon_Johnson 1999

What is the Johnson Model? Association of Intervention Specialists www.
associationofinterventionspecialists.or/what-is-the-johnson-model/2012

DISCUSSION QUESTIONS
FOR SOBER SPRING

ü When Molly goes to see the counselor for the first time, she states she is very nervous. She does not want someone to see her. How often do you think new clients may experience this? How might you address this?

ü The counselor described addiction as being a disease of "denial by many people". Do you agree with this? Who was in "denial" in this story?

ü The disease of addiction is often described as a family disease. It is also one that is progressive which runs in the family. Did we see examples of this in the story?

ü What were some skills that Jack (the counselor) employed that engaged Molly?

ü The Intervention process is described as raising the bottom up. What are your thoughts of this process?

ü Many times in a family where there is active addiction, unacceptable behaviors become "normalized". What are some examples we saw in this story? What are some examples you either have seen or may expect to experience as you move ahead in your career?

ü The counselor and family try to decide if the two youngest children should be included in the actual intervention. What are your thoughts?

ü Molly goes to see her friend in the hospital and she tells him she is going through with the intervention even though she is not sure it is going to work. Josh, her wise friend states, "it already has". What do you think he meant by that?

ü Thoughts about the actual Intervention process as described in the book?

INTERVENTION REACTION PAPER

For this paper we will watch a segment of *Intervention* in class. Prior to this we will have discussed the Intervention process in class as well as discuss the book *Sober Spring*. Your assignment will be to write a reaction paper after watching the segment of *Intervention*. This paper should be no less than two pages and preferably no more than six pages. This paper should include, but not be limited to the following topics:

- What are your thoughts about the Intervention process in general?
- Could you see yourself doing an intervention as part of your practice? Why or why not?
- What were your thoughts of the Intervention episode we viewed in class?
- What, if anything, would you have done different if you were the interventionist?
- What would you say to the identified patient?
- What would you want to say to the family members/loved ones of the identified patient at the beginning of the intervention? At the end?
- What specific clinical issues do you think the identified patient needs to address while in treatment?
- Would you recommend any kind of therapy/services for the family? If so, what?
- Compare and contrast the concepts of interventions as depicted in the A & E show and the book *Sober Spring*. Which do you like better.... why?

Rob Castillo,
LCSW, ICAADC, MISA II
Associate Professor, School of Social Work
Aurora University
347 S. Gladstone Ave.
Aurora, IL 60506
Ph. (630) 844-4570
F. (630) 844-4923

FLIGHT OF THE LOON

DEDICATION

To my Family My Wife, Children, Parents, Brothers and Sisters Of both blood and spirit.

ACKNOWLEDGMENTS

YOU'LL HAVE TO FORGIVE ME. I know that acknowledgments are just supposed to give credit to the people who helped you write a book, but in a way, all of the people I'm about to mention did help me write it.

But, in addition, publishing a book is such a rare opportunity that it is difficult to pass up the chance to thank people who have affected my life, and not just this book.

Everybody should have an Aunt Antoinette. From the time I was little I remember her telling stories about me, my brothers and sister, and my cousins. I heard each of those stories dozens of times, but each time she'd tell one of them her eyes would sparkle and her laughter overflow with love. I don't know if she is where I got my appreciation for stories, but Antoinette certainly helped me know that I am loved not only by her but by my whole extended family.

Another supportive family of mine has been the staff and students at the College of DuPage. I was only twenty-four years old when I started there, and it seems like I grew up there professionally. Through the years, the students and staff have been so nurturing and supportive that I started doing things I never thought I could—like writing stories. I have received lots of help on this one from Rosemary McKinney, Frank Salvatini, Frances Roshier and Lin Bresnahan. They not only were early readers, but taught me a lot about addiction, recovery and eating disorders. Barb Marsh and Judy Czarapata also contributed suggestions and friendship. Cheri Erdman, Rosalyn Long and Beth Ellis read early versions and took the time not only to support me but to suggest specific changes that I made. Beth Ellis and Pat Bodrava helped with typing and Bill Makely with editing.

Several students helped too. Gretchen Puglies, Marlene Fratus, Lydia Wilder, Rita Sullivan, Charlene Keane and Elizabeth O'Flynn read the book and gave me support. Rich Weigel and David Lloyd also read the book, but most of all they provided me with positive models of young people with wisdom beyond their years.

All along I felt God was there-even when I was getting more and more frustrated with how slowly the rewriting and editing was going. Just then Joanne Kutner called and asked me how I was doing. When I shared my frustration, she offered to help and just happened to know well the computer program I was using. A day later my problems were solved.

And finally, thanks to Bill Makely for his help with the second edition of this book, as well as Joe Barillari and April Hanstad for their help and the second chance for the book.

⋅ • ● ● ● ● ● ● ● ● ● ● ● ● ● ● ● ● ● ● ● ⋅

IN MANY WAYS, THAT PARTICULAR evening felt more like fall than spring. The still bare trees were silhouetted sharply against the sliver of red sun that flickered in the western sky. The wind had died away so completely that the lake looked like a silver platter as it mirrored the light gray sky above it. The trees reflected in the glassy water, as did the full, yellow moon swimming on a dark bank of clouds in the east. Sometimes, when the full moon shines on the waters of northern Wisconsin, it appears like so many flickering diamonds. On this night, however, it cut a smooth yellow ribbon right through the center of that silver plate.

The calm waters anticipated the loon long before it touched the surface. Its landing shattered the ribbon into golden kernels—like wheat at harvest.

Soon peace returned as the loon quietly, effortlessly glided through the stillness. Only its small wake disturbed the serenity.

It was early springtime, and as yet there were no crickets or other insects to disturb the hush of the lake. Suddenly the male loon's wail cracked the silence as he summoned his mate. The haunting, half-crazed call of the loon embodied all the beauty and the loneliness of the north country.

Paul Brandt was already in his bedroom. He had excused himself early from the icy tension of the dinner table and hid in his room while his parents continued their argument. He was lying on his bed, thumbing through a bird book, attempting to ignore the yelling. He tried also to ignore the lost and scared feeling inside him. His thin face resting on his rather long, light brown hair on his pillow looked almost like a bird in a nest. His thin, frail body barely made an impression on the mattress where he lay.

From his looks alone it was easy to tell that Paul was quiet and shy. He was the kind of kid about whom teachers would ask themselves at the end of the day, "Was Paul Brandt here today?"

ROBERT F. BOLLENDORF

It had been nearly a year since the Brandt family had confronted Paul's father, Hank, to get him to enter an alcoholism treatment center. The intervention and the subsequent treatment had been successful—at least to the extent that Hank had not drunk alcohol since, as far as Paul knew. But alcohol still played a large part in their family life.

Most of the arguments between Paul's mother, Molly, and Hank still seemed to start because Molly suspected Hank of stopping for a drink or because she resented him running out to AA meetings. Whatever the reason, when they argued, Paul still felt like crawling into a hole to escape. His room was the next best thing.

This night, Paul and his older brother, Ryan, had agreed to open their window to let in some fresh air. The boys were alike in two ways. They both liked sleeping in a cool, almost cold room, and they had similar attitudes about cleanliness.

That attitude was: "Clean only if your mother makes you." So the open window also relieved the smell of sweaty socks and underwear stashed on the floor and under the bed instead of in the clothes hamper.

Paul had probably heard the sound before on other early spring nights when the loons had stopped at the lake outside of town on their way farther north. It was in the more isolated far northern lakes with few or no motor boats that the shy birds made their summer homes and bore their young. But Paul had never really paid attention to the call before. He wasn't even sure the sound came from a bird. He asked Ryan, who was sprawled on the bed next to him, "What made that sound?"

"You should be familiar with that by now," Ryan said.

"That's Mom and Dad fighting."

"Not that, Ryan!" Paul exclaimed. "The animal noise outside."

Just then the loon wailed again.

"That sound!" Paul yelled as he jumped off his bed.

"I thought you were the big bird expert," Ryan mocked.

"That's a loon—just like you." This was the first time anyone suggested that Paul and the loon were brothers. Native Americans believe that all animals are our brothers and sisters, but that we each have a special kinship with only one. Paul had always liked birds, but that night he discovered his relationship with the loon. There was something in that lonely wail that summed up all the feelings he had inside.

120

"What kind of bird is it?" Paul continued with Ryan.

For a change, Ryan was doing homework and began to get irritated with his younger brother. "How should I know, you bird brain. It's like a duck."

Paul began to search his bookshelf thoroughly and went through each of his many books on birds, but he couldn't find a loon.

It wasn't until the next day, when Paul checked with his science teacher, Mr. Jones, that he knew for sure that Ryan wasn't pulling his leg. Mr. Jones showed him a picture of the common loon, with its distinctive black and white markings and bright red eyes that seem to match the craziness of its call.

"You heard them last night too, eh, Paul?" Mr. Jones asked.

Paul was so enamoured with the picture of the loon that it took some time for the question to register. "Oh! Yes," he said,

"I've never heard anything quite like it. How come I've never heard one before?"

"Well, the loons don't stay here. They probably just stopped on their way to their nesting grounds in the lakes north of here."

"Why don't they stay here?" Paul asked.

"Well, in a word, I guess you'd have to say *people*," the teacher responded. "People build cabins and beaches and destroy the marshes and tall grass where loons like to build their nests. Besides, loons are shy, nervous birds and don't like powerboats coming close to them."

Paul began to think more and more that this bird was like him. He too liked to hide out and didn't appreciate people coming close to him with their loud noises. Paul sensed in Mr.

Jones the same kind of connection. The boyish looking young man with a shy smile and glasses too big for his face was a great science teacher, at least as far as Paul was concerned. Mark Jones really knew science and got excited when he spoke about the subject. But he was a timid and inexperienced teacher, and the kids knew it. So discipline in his class was a joke.

Paul once heard two teachers saying, "That's one class that won't need to visit the zoo. They're already in one!"

"Say," Mr. Jones said to Paul, "I belong to the National Preserve the Loon Club. Maybe we could start a chapter here at the school. Would you be interested?"

"Sure," Paul answered. "But why do they need to be protected? Are they endangered?"

"Once there were loons throughout the northern states,"

Mr. Jones replied sadly, "but now only Minnesota has them in abundance." "What would our club do?" Paul asked.

"Well, as a project we could fix up a nesting site on the lake outside of town and see if we couldn't entice two loons to stay here this spring. Some people are having some luck building floating nests that stay out in the water. Loons are excellent swimmers and flyers, but are very clumsy on land because their bodies are built for swimming and diving. Therefore they are attracted to nests that require very little walking and because it offers some protection from bears and coyotes. Then we would have to guard the nest to keep powerboats away from it."

The thought of having the wonderful cry of the loon coming through his open window all summer long inspired Paul. "Let's do it!" he declared with uncharacteristic decisiveness. "How do we start?"

"Well," said Mr. Jones excitedly, "talk to your friends. Let's see if we can generate some more interest."

Paul's shoulders sagged. He didn't have many friends in the junior high, and he certainly didn't see himself as a leader.

As a child, Paul had always been painfully shy, and, while he had made progress in his "social skills" the year since his dad had quit drinking, he was still reluctant to set himself up for rejection.

Yet Paul usually found alternatives to being outgoing, and this situation was no exception.

"How about if I make some posters and then you announce the club in class, Mr. Jones?"

"That sounds fine, Paul," the teacher said gently, for he understood what the earnest young man was struggling with.

"Now you better run so you don't miss the bus."

"Okay," Paul agreed. "See you tomorrow." The teacher grinned as he watched the boy careen down the hallway.

The next day Paul came with his signs and Mr. Jones made his announcement in class. The response was less enthusiastic than they both had hoped, but it was about what they should have expected. Only three other kids joined—all loners like Paul. The three probably joined more to identify with something or someone than from a real commitment to saving loons. Nor was the membership likely to increase, since the club quickly became known around the school as "the Loonies."

Undaunted by their reputation, however, the club members began their mission the following weekend when they visited the lake and walked around the shore looking for the best possible nesting site for a pair of loons.

IT DOESN'T TAKE LONG FOR word about unusual behavior to spread through a small town. Soon everyone knew about the Loonies. Most folks just smiled. A few school board members, however, were angry that one of their teachers had become the subject of ridicule. A few people even supported the efforts of Paul and his friends, although they did so silently.

Around the Brandt kitchen table, the Loonies provoked new arguments—ones, at least, that involved new participants and weren't about alcohol or AA meetings.

"Even though you're still in junior high, we've already heard the whole story at the high school," Ryan complained to Paul. "I don't like being ridiculed because of you and your stupid loons."

Paul sat quietly staring at the floor while his brother continued. "You know, me and my friends go to the lake all the time to go boating and swimming. I'm already dreading the warm weather. We'll go to the beach and there you'll be with your geek friends doing God knows what with some goofy looking birds."

"That goes double for me," their sister Sally added. "Word travels fast in grade school, too, and it's twice as hard to get people to like you when people are making fun of your older brother. Someone called me a loon balloon the other day."

"Oh lighten up, you two!" Bobbie, the elder sister protested. "I think it's neat that Paul's excited about something.

Your precious popularity will survive."

"That's easy for you to say, Bobbie," Ryan countered.

"You're graduating in a few weeks. Me, I have to return to that school in the fall."

Hank leaned back in his chair and spoke for the first time.

"Well, Molly," he said, "you claim I'm not recovering, but look at me! Right now I'm doing all I can to 'let go and let God' instead of jumping in and ending this argument."

"Hank, when it comes to these kids you've been letting go since they were babies," Molly shot back sarcastically.

The kids all looked quickly over at Hank. He just smiled, and the tension was relieved—for now, at least.

About a week later came the first really warm day of spring.

The water in the lake was still far too cold for swimming, but the sun was bright. As it baked the sand, it seemed ready and waiting to thaw bones chilled by the long winter.

Ryan and his friends staked out their usual headquarters on the shore at the Roper place. John Roper's father was a prominent attorney and school board member, and his mother ran the clothing store in town. John was their only child and they spoiled him terribly. The Ropers lived on the lake and they had a private beach where they docked a huge speedboat. The teenage boys liked the spot, because they weren't subject to the rules of the public beach next door. Yet only a small fence separated them from it, so they could still conveniently check out the girls.

That morning, the band of highschool boys worked hard to put the Roper's dock in the water and to launch the boat for the season. Both of John's parents were away at meetings, so the boys had also downed a few beers. Now that their work was finished, they were lying on the dock and entertaining themselves by commenting on which of the girls sunbathing on the beach had picked up a few pounds over the winter. They also had great fun at the expense of the Loonies, who were out in a small dinghy trying to anchor some buoys and their new nest. As was usually the case, John Roper led the assault.

Roper—which is what everyone called him—was quite large. He looked like he might be a linebacker on the football team, but in fact most of his afternoons during the school year were spent in detentions. Roper had short, cropped black hair, piercing brown eyes and a pockmarked face that completed his linebacker appearance.

Mark Jones was supervising the Loonies as they carefully tried to drop anchors that would secure the buoys, each buoy carrying a sign that read: "Loon Preserve. No Wake."

Roper commented to Ryan, "Maybe when Paul gets done with his loon posters, he can come over to the beach and post a 'Save the Whale' sign for when your sister Sally goes swimming."

"Button it, Roper. Don't even mention those two to me,"

Ryan replied. Ryan was smaller than Roper, but like most of the Brandt males, except for Paul, he had an athletic looking body, which had developed considerably over the last year.

Ryan had a rugged strength that his friends respected. He would talk tough, just like Roper, but there was rarely any menace in his words.

"Roper, you're just bitter because some girl who has yet to lose her baby fat has probably spurned your pitiful advances,"

Zack said playfully. Zack Pierce was Ryan's best friend. They had been friends since grade school. There was a time when Zack would have been right in the middle of ridiculing others and involved in the beer drinking. But that was before he had been arrested for driving under the influence of alcohol and his parents had forced him to get help for what he admitted had become a problem. In spite of Zack's early resentment at being confronted with being an alcoholic at such a young age, the treatment had "taken hold" and he was staying sober. In conversations with Ryan, Zack credited the addictions treatment center at the local hospital and Alcoholics Anonymous with turning his life around.

Zack was now a member of the swim team and very conscientious about school. In many ways he no longer fit in with this particular group, and he probably wouldn't hang out with them if Ryan wasn't there. Zack avoided situations where there was drinking unless, like today, there was plenty of open space and other activities for him to be involved. Since he had quit drinking alcohol and using drugs, Zack's surfer-boy face had taken on a peaceful and gentle appearance that matched his new personality. But he remained one person who was not intimidated by Roper.

"Oh, Zack, I forgot you were here," Roper said in mock contrition. "I guess it's because you never have diddly to say until someone says something critical of one of the Brandts."

Roper tried to sound as playful as Zack, but the tension in their relationship rose icily to the surface.

"We never have to worry about forgetting you're around, do we Roper?" Zack fired back.

"Hey, we did all this work getting the boat in the water," said Steve Johnson, another one of the gang of boys, changing the subject. "Are we ever going to take it out, or are we going to lie on this beach listening to you guys bicker all afternoon?"

"Yeah!" Roper yelled. "Let's go swamp the Loonies."

Few people got as much enjoyment out of disturbing other people as did John Roper.

He raced down the dock and jumped into the boat. The others followed with much less enthusiasm. When they were aboard, Roper started the powerful inboard motor and quickly backed out of the dock, heading for the other side of the lake where the Loonies were setting the buoys.

Paul, along with Mark Jones and two other members of the club, were struggling in a small dinghy with the heavy anchors that would hold the buoys in place. The ice had melted off the lake only a few weeks earlier, so none of them were eager to get wet.

They were leaning over the edge, putting in one of the anchors, when Roper's big inboard went speeding by not five feet from them. In a moment, they were all in the cold water.

As Paul found himself struggling to the surface, the first thing he felt was a band tightening around his chest—his muscles constricting from the cold. Paul wasn't sure he'd be able to breathe even if he made it to the surface. When he finally broke the water, the others were already up and swimming the short distance to shore. Mr. Jones turned to see if Paul was all right.

"Can you swim?" he managed to ask.

"I think so," Paul said, gasping for air.

Luckily for the freezing Loonies, the day had started out cool but had gradually warmed. They had each started the day in long pants and sweatshirts but had peeled off layers of clothes.

By the time they had been dumped overboard they were all in shorts and t-shirts. Now they were able to take off their wet clothes and replace them with dry, warm ones. The spring sun and the dry clothes soon helped their shivering to subside.

Nothing helped their sense of humiliation and frustration.

Roper slowed the boat long enough to make sure each of the Loonies made it to shore safely, then he laughed and sped toward the public beach.

"Smart move, Roper," Zack yelled sarcastically. "There was a teacher in that boat. Are you looking to get expelled?"

"You mean Jones, the king of the Loonies and the wimps?" Roper replied. "He wouldn't report us even if it had happened in school—while it didn't. The Loonies are not a schoolsponsored club. My dad would just love to have an excuse to get rid of that jerk. Just let him try to make trouble. He and that club are an embarrassment to the school and this town.

We just did everyone a favor."

"Wow! Look." Steve again redirected the conversation.

"Michelle got a new bikini over the winter. Let's get a closer look. Swing by the beach."

Ryan was noticeably quiet. He hoped that this experience would get Paul off his loon kick, but he also hoped Paul wouldn't go home and tell Hank. His father always seemed to be just waiting for an excuse to jump on Ryan's case.

"Hey, Michelle. How about a ride?" Roper yelled toward the beach. She ignored him, as she always did.

Meanwhile Paul sat on the shore, still shivering every once in a while. "Those guys are in trouble now," he exclaimed.

"What are you going to do to them, Mr. Jones?"

"Nothing," the teacher answered quietly.

"But Mr. Jones, we could have drowned out there!" Paul stammered. "I know, Paul, and it was a very stupid thing for them to do," Mr. Jones responded gently. "But to make an issue of it would only cause more ridicule for what we're trying to do. Do you want that?"

"No, but . . ." Paul paused. He wanted to say more, but he gave in to Mr. Jones's superior logic. Paul was confused.

Sometimes, he thought, grown-ups can make things sound right even when they don't seem right.

Paul decided that he wouldn't say anything at home, either.

If he did, his dad would just yell at Ryan as usual. It would end with the whole family being mad at Paul for causing trouble.

He'd just have to get even with Ryan by making him wonder whether or not he'd tell. Since Ryan was used to being in trouble, however, Paul wasn't sure how effective that tactic would be.

All this scheming just made his head hurt. It was bad enough being cold, without having a headache too.

CHAPTER **3**

• • • • • • • • • • ● • • • • • • • • • • • •

SALLY WAS SUNBATHING WITH HER friends on the public beach and had watched as Roper swamped the Loonies. She let out a gasp as she saw Paul thrown into the water, but once she saw him reach shore safely, she joined in the laughter with all her friends. Their delight increased as they watched the big speedboat head toward them.

The young girls, just entering adolescence, thought high school boys were gods, and Sally thought John Roper, with all his confidence and power, was the best.

Though the water was still quite cold, her excitement and her few pounds of extra insulation allowed her to wade out past her knees to welcome the boys like a tropical island girl whose men had just returned from a long, successful fishing venture.

The boys, though, were concentrating on Michelle Lawrence in her new bathing suit and hardly noticed Sally until they realized that Michelle was snubbing them.

Things had changed for Sally in the past year, not so much because of the intervention with Sally's father and his stopping drinking, but just because she was reaching the age when things change quickly for young girls. In the Brandt family, she was still the joker who often had everyone bending over in laughter, and she brought that same skill to her friendships.

Sally had lots of friends, and because she was funny, the other girls enjoyed being around her. That had always been true.

What was changing were the bodies of those friends—that, and the fact that the subject of boys crept more and more into their endless phone conversations. Boys were suddenly the main focus of the girls' pointing and giggling during school and their long exchanges while walking home and sitting on each others' porches.

But Sally's body was not changing—at least not as far as she could tell. It was still the cute little round body that seemed to fit so well with her comedian personality but not at all with the prospect of attracting a boy's attention.

The only boy Sally felt totally comfortable with was Paul.

Though they were very different—or maybe because of that— they had always been close. Sally had always made fun of her brother, and, no matter how biting the humor, he always just smiled. If they were alone, the two talked easily, and Paul often had interesting things to say, though she rarely told him that.

The other day, for example, Paul had said he noticed that, though she could still make people laugh, more and more often her jokes seemed to be at her own expense. He said she was drawing attention to herself as a defense against her own pain. That night at a sleepover with friends, Sally had looked at herself in the mirror in front of the others, raised her wrist to her forehead and sighed, "Puberty has passed me by." That got a laugh out of her friends, but Paul's words rang in her ears.

Sally was at a point in her life when her fat was no longer just baby fat. It was fat. Even though she wasn't very overweight, next to her taller, slimmer friends she stood out. Though she didn't let on, she hated being the "perky, pudgy" one.

Among the Brandt family, sensitive issues were discussed, but never honestly or directly. Everything was fair game— especially where Sally was concerned— as long as it was in the form of a joke.

So as the speedboat went by her, it was natural for Ryan and his friends to shout: "Whale off the starboard bow. Man the harpoons!"

Then they all laughed. Sally, being ever quick to join in, scooped up some of the cold water and sucked it into her mouth, blowing it out like a whale uses its blowhole. The boys and her friends laughed all the louder.

When Paul and Sally met on the way home from the lake that afternoon, they both walked quietly for a while. Finally, Sally spoke.

"So, will you give up on this silly project of yours now, Paul?" she asked.

"No way, Sally," Paul shot back with a fierceness contrary to his nature. "If it's so embarrassing to you to have me protect a few helpless birds, you'll just have to live with it."

"I'm sorry, Paul," she said. "Actually, it's me I find most embarrassing right now, and I need your help with it."

"What do you mean, Sally?" Paul asked. "You're confusing me."

Sally went on to describe what had happened at the beach, and how the boys' words and laughter had felt like real harpoons, and how each had hurt her deeply. She then went on to describe her plan for losing weight.

"I'm going to join the track team at school. That way I won't have to eat dinner with the rest of the family. I'll tell Mom to save me just a salad because my stomach is all jumbled from running. I'll tell her I'm eating a big lunch at school and I'm not that hungry at dinner."

"Why can't you just go on a regular diet or just eat less?" Paul asked.

"Because Mom thinks I'm too young for diets, and besides they don't work for me. Once I start to eat I have trouble stopping. The only thing that works for me is to skip meals."

Sally's voice sounded more and more pleading.

"Paul, would you get up and run with me in the morning?" she asked. "I can tell Mom I need to do it for track and that you're going with me to keep me company and for the exercise."

"Oh, Sally, I hate running!" Paul whined. "I use any excuse I can to get out of it in gym class."

"Please, Paul! I know I won't get up on my own, but with your help I could do it." Sally grabbed his arm and raised her right hand for emphasis. "I promise I won't bug you about the loons and I'll even stick up for you against Ryan."

"I don't think Ryan will say much anyway," Paul replied wryly. "He knows if he does I'll tell Dad what happened today and that they were drinking to boot."

"Will you do it for me, Paul?" Sally begged.

"Okay," Paul finally conceded, "but only till you're in the habit and can do it on your own. And you have to promise not to tell Mom and Dad what happened today."

Neither Sally nor Paul said a word at dinner that night about the dunking, and Ryan spent the night waiting for the shoe that never dropped. Paul avoided Ryan and didn't even look at his brother during dinner, which seemed to bug Ryan more than usual.

Paul felt good about giving his brother the silent treatment, although that night he had bad dreams that all involved not being able to breathe.

So he wasn't sorry when morning came, even though it meant he had to keep his promise to Sally to go running. It was cold, and Paul complained the entire time it took them to go around the block twice. Sally had to stop and walk a lot, which didn't bother Paul at all. She tried to talk him into a third trip, but it had turned even colder and Paul said, "I'm going in."

"At least we did it," she said as she followed him inside.

●●●●●●●●●●●●●●●●●●●●●●●

DESPITE THE ABUSE THEY RECEIVED from people in school and the town, the Loonies persisted in their attempts to establish a nesting site. Maybe it was because, for kids used to being totally ignored, negative attention was better than none at all. Or perhaps it was because they soon saw their efforts rewarded. A pair of loons nested on the lake.

The Loonies took turns watching the birds. During one of Paul's watches, the female loon laid an egg in the nest. Paul felt as though he were a part of the family—an older brother maybe. He began coming to the nesting site even when it wasn't his turn to observe.

It was on one of his regular days, a Saturday, that it happened. It was a cloudy day, but warm and humid. Paul had gotten tired of lying on his stomach watching the loons through the binoculars and had rolled over onto his back. He didn't need to watch them constantly. He had learned to tell what was happening from their different calls. At the moment, the female was sitting on the nest while the male was out fishing.

They communicated back and forth with short, soft, little calls that sounded like hoots.

Then Paul heard the male use the tremolo—the laughing sound that loons make when they are frightened.

As soon as he rolled over, he saw why.

Roper's speedboat was heading straight towards the loon.

It quickly dived to avoid the boat and to divert it from the nest.

The tactic worked momentarily as Roper slowed down to see where the loon had gone.

Roper had ignored the "No Wake" signs and had charged the male at full speed. The wake from the boat began to wash up on shore. Loons, though very agile in water, are clumsy on land. With legs far back on their bodies, they are great divers but terrible walkers. Because of this, they build their nests right at the edge of the water, and the wake from passing speedboats disturbs them greatly.

As the wake began splashing the nest, the female waddled into the water and began flapping her wings and running on the surface of the water until she had enough speed to get airborne. She then flew away from Roper's boat—partly from fear but also to lead the intruder away from the nest.

The male loon finally surfaced out near the middle of the lake and Roper and his friends quickly gave chase. Having accomplished his diversion mission and having the room this time he needed for his long take-off, the male also took flight. Paul watched as the male skimmed the water with the speedboat closing in. The bird gained altitude before the boat could catch him.

Paul turned his attention back toward the nest, but he was too late. The damage had been done. The chick would not be born. A gull had landed in the unprotected nest, pecked a hole in the shell and was now greedily devouring the insides. Paul screamed and waved his arms, but it was in vain.

The male and female returned to the nest at the same time.

Paul heard their familiar wail for what he thought would be the last time that summer. It sounded sadder and lonelier than ever, but perhaps that was because it echoed his own feelings as tears streamed down his cheeks.

Paul was not the only one who observed the boat chasing the loons. Ryan had been lying on Roper's dock and watched as the boat had sped inside the buoys. He had seen his brother stand up in the weeds and wave his arms, but he didn't know why. Roper and the boys in the boat knew only that they had scared the male bird.

Paul wanted to walk over to Roper's house and confront them all. He had even picked up a stick to use to make his point. As he got closer, however, he saw the boys pop the tops on cans of beer as they climbed laughing from the boat. The sound of the cans opening brought back the dread that Paul used to feel when his father would open a beer in the middle of a tirade. Suddenly Paul's rage turned to fear and he stopped in his tracks.

He returned to the loon site to find Mark Jones staring into the nest. Through his clenched teeth Paul told his teacher the whole story.

"Well, maybe it's for the best," Mr. Jones said sadly. "It's still early. The loons can still fly to a new nesting site and still have a chick this year. Maybe loons don't belong on this lake.

It's just too busy."

"But I want them on this lake!" Paul shouted.

Mark Jones smiled. He liked this intense young man.

"Loons and people don't mix, Paul," he said. His voice was calm.

"We don't get along with people either, but we can't just fly away," Paul fired back. He didn't even notice he had said "we" but Mr. Jones did.

"Perhaps we can learn from the loon to accept that there are battles we just can't win," Mr. Jones answered in the same gentle voice. "The loon has survived for millions of years.

Perhaps that's one reason. It knows when to retreat."

"I don't want to survive if I have to spend my life retreating."

Paul said angrily.

He ran home, leaving Mark Jones to decide what to do with the egg that would never hatch. Paul went straight to his room, knowing Ryan would be home soon. He waited behind the door.

RYAN LEFT FOR HOME SHORTLY after Paul. "Stick around and have another beer," Roper said. "We'll wait for the loons to settle down again, then we'll take another shot at them."

"No, I'd better get home and stay in good with my old man so I can go out tonight," Ryan answered.

"Why not just stay here and drink right through dinner?

Then you'll already be out and your old man can't make you stay home." This was Roper's logic after several beers.

"But once I did get home, he might keep me there all summer," Ryan tried uselessly to reason.

"You've become a real worrier, Brandt," Roper answered.

"You don't drink as much, you hardly ever get detentions anymore, and I end up sitting in the dean's office by myself.

You've become almost as big a wimp as your friend Zack. Next, you'll be joining the Pep Club at school."

To add to his embarrassment, Ryan had to get on his bike and pedal home. He had a driver's license, but his sister and mother were using the second car that afternoon.

"Now be careful with your bike in traffic," he heard Roper mock as he rode away.

When Ryan got home, he went directly to his room, afraid that his mother might smell the beer on his breath.

When he walked through the door, Paul sprang at him. His agile little body felt more like a distracting insect to Ryan than the mountain lion Paul wished he were. He didn't even knock Ryan down. Ryan simply bent his back and gave a little twist and it was Paul who landed on the floor. He tried to struggle to his feet, but Ryan was quickly on top of him. Ryan pinned down Paul's arms and legs.

Ryan's voice was angry, but he spoke in hushed tones so as not to attract his mother's attention. "What's the matter with you, you little jerk?"

Paul didn't try to be so quiet. "You killed the . . ."

Ryan quickly covered Paul's mouth.

"Shut up!"

Their mother was quick to detect the sharp voices, even from downstairs.

"What's going on up there?" Molly called from the bottom of the stairs.

"Nothing," Ryan managed to answer calmly. "I just tripped on some junk by the door."

"Maybe you should clean that pigsty so you don't kill yourself," Molly called, returning to her work in the kitchen.

Ryan whispered closely into Paul's ear, "I'll take my hand from your mouth, if you promise to talk quietly."

Paul tried to bite the hand, but Ryan held his mouth shut.

Then, though he wanted so much to continue being strong, Paul began to cry in spite of himself.

When Ryan slowly took his hand from Paul's mouth, Paul whispered angrily, "You killed the chick."

"What are you talking about?" Ryan asked, genuinely confused. "I wasn't even in the boat. Besides, they never went near the nest."

"The wake from the boat scared away the mother. While she was gone, a seagull ate the egg. You might as well have gone over and stepped on it," Paul sobbed, as again his tears betrayed him.

"I'm sorry, Paul. Really I am. But how were they supposed to know that would happen?" Ryan's voice sounded sincere.

"They didn't have to know," Paul blurted, the words tripping over each other in his anger. "All they had to do was obey the stupid 'No Wake' signs and let the loons alone. What had they done to anybody? What had we done to anybody? Now their baby's dead and they'll leave for sure."

Paul forgot about his mother and screamed, "I hope you're all happy!"

Ryan again covered his brother's mouth. "I didn't like the club, Paul. I admit it. But I'm sorry about the loons and their baby." Ryan's voice again sounded sympathetic.

"I know you're mad at me because they're my friends, but I wasn't even in the boat. What did you expect me to do?" He took his hand away again.

"Even if you were with them you wouldn't have stopped them," Paul sniffed. "I didn't see you throwing yourself overboard to stop them when they swamped us a few weeks back."

"You're right, I probably wouldn't have," Ryan admitted.

"And I appreciate the fact that you didn't tell Dad. But Paul, why do you have to get so upset about some stupid birds?"

Ryan sounded truly confused.

"Why do you care about such stupid friends?" Paul responded.

It was an impasse and they both knew it. "Okay," Ryan answered. "I'll say it again-I'm sorry it happened. If I let you up, do you promise not to tell Mom or Dad?"

"Yeah," Paul said. "But just stay away from me and keep your freaking friends away too. Better yet, put them in a cage somewhere."

Ryan wanted to laugh and rub his knuckles through Paul's hair, but he thought better of it. He was pretty sure Paul knew they had been drinking at Roper's house, and he didn't want to upset Paul enough to tell their parents. He let Paul up and walked out of the room, respecting his brother's desire to be left alone.

After the egg was destroyed, the rest of the club gave up on the loons. Paul continued to work on the site, hoping the loons would stay, or at least come back the next year. Mr. Jones took the empty egg to science class to show why people shouldn't make a wake near a loon's nest, but that just gave his students another reason to make fun of him and the Loonies.

The last act of the club, led by Paul, was to steal the egg from the classroom and bury it near the nesting site. They put a cross on it with the inscription:

"Here's a life that will never be, because of John Roper's stupidity."

But they hid the grave in the weeds and wrote their message small because they were afraid Roper might find it.

IT WAS THE FIRST ANNIVERSARY of Hank's sobriety. He had had one little bracer that Molly didn't know about before going to see the counselor the day of the intervention. That had been his last drink.

Hank stopped at the hardware store on his way home from work to pick up some things he needed for a project Molly had been bugging him to finish. He met up with someone he knew from AA and they decided to go to the bakery for a cup of coffee and a sweet roll to celebrate Hank's anniversary. Hank got home a few minutes late, and he could tell that Molly was tense, although she tried to ask pleasantly where he had been.

Sarcastically, Hank replied, "I stopped by the bar and had a few drinks to celebrate my one year of sobriety, Nosey. I wanted to accept my medallion at the meeting tonight with a buzz on."

"I was just asking, Hank," Molly said defensively.

"Yeah, yeah, I know," Hank said sadly. "And you have no business asking. God, Molly, it's been a year. When are you going to let it go?"

"Hank, for ten years I waited almost every night with a house full of kids, not knowing where you were or when you'd get home," Molly replied with a combination of anger and sadness in her voice. "So you'll have to excuse me if I have a little problem forgetting. I do my best."

"How long are you going to make me suffer for those things I can't change, Molly?" he replied with his own mixed feelings of anger and hopelessness. "Do you have any idea how hard each day is?"

Hank went off to read the paper and settle down before dinner, while Molly finished preparing it. She had made his favorite meal and even a little cake with one candle to celebrate.

Sally had started track practice and wouldn't be home for dinner and Ryan had a part-time job at the supermarket. The oldest son, Scott, was away at college, so it was just Hank, Molly, Bobbie and Paul who sat down at the dinner table.

Paul wished Sally were there to crack a few jokes to ease the tension. When Hank saw the dinner and the cake, however, he kissed Molly on the cheek and said, "Thanks, Moll," and a pleasant conversation followed. After the meal they ate cake and sang "Happy Anniversary to You." Hank seemed to Paul to be nervous but appreciative of the fuss.

They had finished the cake when Bobbie asked the question only she could get away with, "Daddy, what has it been like for you the last year?"

Hank sat back in his chair for a moment. Paul thought his father seemed surprised at the candor of the question, but he also seemed lost in thought. Paul's first impulse was to excuse himself, but his curiosity for once overruled his fear of conflict.

"Well, I'm going to an AA meeting tonight, and my sponsor is going to present me with my one-year medallion," he finally responded, "I'm proud of that, but it is the first time in a while that I have looked forward to going to a meeting. It seems too seldom that people get recognized at a meeting for doing good things. People in AA always seem to focus on their problems. All I seem to hear about is either problems getting sober or problems staying sober, and I'm tired of problems. Life never seems to be much fun anymore.

"To tell you the truth," Hank continued, "I don't miss the taste of alcohol. My craving for alcohol seemed to disappear after a month or so. But I find myself more and more forgetting the bad times that alcohol caused and remembering more and more the good times. My sponsor tells me that this too shall pass and just keep going to meetings, but I'm getting pretty tired of them."

Paul thought how nice it was to hear his dad talk quietly about things rather than yell about them like he always used to.

"You seemed real excited when you first got out of treatment, Dad." Paul couldn't believe he had made such a direct observation about his father's recovery. The ease of his Dad's response was even more surprising to him.

"Oh, yeah, when I left treatment I was really gung ho for sobriety and for going to meetings," Hank replied with a laugh.

"I got a sponsor while I was still in the treatment center, and I would talk to him daily on the telephone. Now, I and your mother fight about me going to another meeting like we used to fight about me going to the bar."

Molly started to react but then thought better of it. "The honeymoon is over, I guess," Hank continued. "It seems to me that having a sponsor is like having a second wife: 'Did you get to a meeting?' 'Have you had quiet time today?' 'How are you coming on your fourth step?' I have a wife to nag me; I don't need a sponsor too!"

"But Hank, what do you want from me?" Molly had contained herself as long as she could. "Can't you accept that your life has changed and these are things you need to do to make it successful?"

"First of all, Molly, I can't believe you're asking me that, when you don't accept the things you need to do to make your own life successful," Hank shot back. Molly picked up some dishes and went to the sink. Everyone fell silent.

Finally, Hank changed the subject: "To tell you the truth, Bobbie, I'd like to be able to drink socially like so many other people do, and I resent people who seem to be able to do so.

My brother, Ken, for instance, can stop at a bar now and then with the guys from the construction company and have a few beers. He always makes excuses for me because we both know I can't join him. Even if I told myself I would only drink a soda, in my heart I know better. Once at the bar, it would be like old times and I know that with all the other guys sitting around drinking beer, I would want one too."

Molly's face turned ashen, but she continued to listen. "So I drive home or go to a meeting instead," Hank said, "but I miss going out with the guys I work with. People at the meetings laugh and joke, but it's not the same. In all honesty, what I miss most is that simply by bending my elbow and putting a cold beer to my mouth I could end all my cares and feel on top of the world. When I was in a bar the tensions of the day disappeared— literally. They just floated away."

Molly kept clearing the table. She was visibly agitated.

Paul and Bobbie sat riveted to their chairs. They had never heard their father talk this way.

"Then there is the problem with feelings," he went on.

"Everyone is always wanting to know how I feel. I drank so I wouldn't have to know how I felt. Now, everyone wants to know about my feelings. Then when I do take the time to check how I'm feeling, I find I am usually depressed, lonely or angry.

So what's the use of knowing?"

Now it was Molly's turn to speak. She came up behind her husband and put her hands on his shoulders.

"You know, Hank, this is the first time in a year that we've really talked openly about this kind of thing," she said gently. "I don't like everything I hear, but I can handle it. Maybe I can even help.

Why don't you let me in more?"

"It seems to me you don't want just to know," Hank replied steadily. "You want to control. When Bobbie asked me about this past year, I heard concern and interest. When you ask, I hear meddling and accusation."

"Hank, for years I was home with little kids and no one to talk to," Molly began, leaving her hands where they were.

Hank rolled his eyes, thinking he'd heard this speech before, but it took a new twist.

"I so much enjoyed it early in our marriage when you would come home from work, and we'd talk and I'd tell you about cute little things the kids did," Molly said. "Then, when you started coming home later and later, my disappointment turned to anger. Then we'd fight, and that was the last thing I wanted. Now, even though the kids are big and I have lots of people to talk to, I still look forward to seeing my husband walk through the back door. Since you've quit drinking I've discovered a new feeling when you don't come home. I feel rejected."

Hank was silent for a while. "How do things get so screwed up, Molly?" he asked gently. "You were always my favorite person to talk to, too." He smiled and took her hand.

"I'd like it to be that way again."

"I'll try harder, Hank," Molly said, sitting down next to him and looking into his eyes for the first time in a long time.

"So will I," he answered tenderly.

Paul and Bobbie slipped from the room.

CHAPTER 7

· • • • • • • • • ● ● ● ● ● ● ● ● • • • • • • · ·

THOUGH MOLLY AND PASTOR BROOKS had been acquainted for many years, it was through their mutual friend, Dr. Joshua Krueger, that they had become real friends. Josh had been a quiet man who loved music. Besides being the town's doctor, he had also been the song leader for the pastor and Molly's congregation. His courage in facing his own illness and death had helped give Molly the strength she needed to go through with Hank's intervention and had led Pastor Brooks to change his own life radically.

Josh Krueger's love for music was truly contagious.

After Josh's death, the pastor had appointed Molly the church's music director and became her assistant. Although he didn't have Josh's sweet tenor voice, he could still carry a tune. And nothing helped him express his feelings more fully than music.

All his adult life, John Brooks had been a man who lived through his intellect. His mind was not in the clouds, it was in the heavens. He had looked down on people with a distant curiosity and provided only a sterile spirituality to the parishioners who brought him the problems of their lives.

But Josh Krueger had changed all that. He had talked openly with his pastor—indeed the entire congregation— about his illness and coming death, sharing his fears and his regrets. Josh's openness enabled his friend to become more aware of his own feelings. These feelings started with the pastor's own loneliness and fear, but then became true empathy for the people who came to him for guidance. While he never lost his intellectual curiosity, his focus changed. He began to read books about people and how to help them. He studied counseling and psychology. He became interested in 12-step programs like Alcoholics Anonymous and Al-Anon in which many of his parishioners participated. He even began to attend those groups' open public information meetings to learn more directly what they had to offer.

Over the past year following Josh's death, Pastor Brooks had gradually taken over the role of Molly's friend and confidant that had previously been Josh's. In Pastor Brooks, Molly found a person who was not only understanding but excited about the intervention with her husband she had organized and the changes that had followed.

After the scene on Hank's anniversary, and with Pastor Brook's encouragement, Molly again committed herself to change. "Each day, I tell myself I'll be different," Molly confided to the minister as she sat at the organ while they practiced the hymns for that coming Sunday. "I really thought that after the intervention life would be easy. I never expected this. I hear 'Let go and let God' in Al-Anon all the time, but all the silly slogans don't make it happen. I've tried, but I can't let go."

"Molly, that saying is just talking about the same faith in God that you've been encouraged to have ever since you were a child in religion class," Pastor Brooks replied. "You are being asked to believe that God has a plan for you. Your job is to accept and follow the plan, not manufacture it."

"Okay, then, what about the expression, 'Pray as if everything depended on God and act as if everything depended on you'?" Molly challenged.

"That's still good theology, Molly, but you're overdoing the last part," the pastor replied. "You're trying to act for Hank, not just yourself, and you can't do that."

"My head understands, John. I just wish I could convince my heart," Molly relented. "Do you think God will forgive me for what I'm doing to my husband and family?"

"Forgive you for what?" Pastor Brooks asked. "For loving them too much? For wanting the best for them and trying to make it happen?"

Molly sat silently for a few minutes. Then she stood abruptly and started for the church door.

"Tonight, I'm going to bring back the love and romance that was once present in our marriage," she announced with an uncharacteristic giggle. "I think a little party for two is in order to celebrate a year of recovery."

"Well, don't expect too much from one night, Molly," her friend warned. "Your problems didn't start in one night, and they probably won't end that quickly, either."

But Molly didn't seem to hear. She left quickly as though she were on a mission.

That night was a Friday, and Paul ate dinner alone. Molly and Hank had eaten early so Hank could get to a meeting, and the other children were all out at friends' houses for the night.

After he had eaten, Paul was anxious to take advantage of the fact that he practically had the bathroom to himself. With five kids and only one bathroom, no one in the Brandt family had the luxury of taking much time in the bathroom—except at rare times like these. His mom was home, but she always took showers and was in and out in no time. So when Paul found the door locked, he waited outside, confident she'd be right out. When he heard water running into the tub—the sound of someone taking a bath—he knocked on the door. "Sally, is that you?" Paul called quizzically.

"No," Molly answered. "It's your mother."

"Will you be out soon?" Paul asked, surprised.

"I'll probably be a while," Molly answered.

Paul walked away feeling confused as well as uncomfortable.

After her bath, Molly powdered her body and put on her makeup. Then she took a long look at herself in the mirror. She saw a woman who was remarkably resilient, considering she had had five children and was over forty. But a longer, closer look told the rest of the story. She saw lines, sagging skin and varicose veins. Molly shrugged. She liked her body. Besides, she had earned every wrinkle.

She put on the negligee she found in the bottom of her dresser drawer and the long lacy robe that went over it. When Paul walked by her after she finally opened the bathroom door he was sure he was seeing a mirage. But enough reality sunk in for him to know he should make himself scarce.

On his way back from the bathroom, Paul could see his mother reading in the living room. He became curious how his dad would react. The AA meeting had started at 7:30 and usually lasted an hour, so Paul began listening for him at about

9:00. By 9:30, when Hank still wasn't home, he could hear his mother begin to rustle the pages of her book, and he heard the long sighs that usually signalled aggravation. At 10:30, he heard her heading up the stairs to bed, even though he knew she wouldn't sleep.

Molly had just turned out the bedroom lights when Hank walked in. "Another celebration?" she spat out, not even trying to hide her irritation.

Paul felt guilty for listening through the bedroom wall, but curiosity got the best of him.

Hank sounded surprised. "Molly! I expected you to be in bed. I didn't realize you'd be waiting up for me. I thought the kids . . ."

She quickly walked over to him and gently put her hand to his mouth.

"I'm sorry I snapped, Hank," she whispered. "I didn't want it to be this way. Let's go to bed. Paul's asleep, and the others are staying with friends."

Paul shut his eyes tight. He had invaded their privacy and didn't want to hear the sounds from his parents' bedroom. For a while, everything was quiet, but all too soon he heard a noise he didn't expect. He heard the bedroom door opening and his father's frustrated voice saying, "Now there's nothing between us that works anymore!" Then Paul heard the door slam.

Then from the bedroom he heard his mother's sad voice calling, "I shouldn't have rushed you, Hank. It's okay. It'll be better next time."

In his heart, Paul knew it really wasn't okay. Things were not fine, and they certainly wouldn't get better tonight nor tomorrow. He began to wonder about ever.

CHAPTER 8

As he looked back on the days that followed, Paul was convinced that it was God's will that kept the loons on the same site and that allowed the mother loon to lay not one but two more eggs. It must also have been God who put the praying mantises where he and Mark Jones could observe them.

Paul was at the loon site with his teacher on the day after the incident in his parents' bedroom. Paul was tired. He hadn't gotten much sleep the night before. He had never given sex much thought. It wasn't that he didn't know the facts of life.

He knew where those two eggs came from that the mother and father loon guarded so closely. He had watched birds and other animals mate. It always seemed so natural. But humans were complicated. They didn't have sex just during mating season.

His brother Ryan seemed to be in constant heat, judging from the way he talked about girls and how he looked at the magazines he smuggled into their room. How could humans take such a simple, natural thing and mess it up so badly?

Paul watched a girl water-skiing in the middle of the lake.

She wore a bikini and was pleasant enough to look at, but he didn't get the urges that Ryan talked about. He wondered if he ever would—or if he wanted to after hearing what he had the night before. Paul had the feeling that something had gone very wrong for his parents, but he couldn't understand how they could fail at expressing love.

"You seem preoccupied today, Paul," Mr. Jones finally said.

Paul didn't answer. It took a long time for the comment even to filter into his thoughts. Then Paul was even more distracted, trying to decide whether he could bring all this up to a teacher. And if he did, what questions would he ask?

That was when Mr. Jones saw the praying mantises.

"Look!" he said excitedly to Paul. "They're mating. Let's see how good a lover he is." The two snuck closer. They watched as the relatively smaller male mounted the larger female. The whole act took only a matter of moments. When it was over, the male dismounted and moved away.

"He must have been good," Mr. Jones commented wryly.

Paul thought for a few seconds. There must be a lot more to this sex thing than he thought. How could Mr. Jones tell anything about the praying mantises mating technique from what they had just seen? He finally got up the nerve to ask.

"How could you tell he was good, Mr. Jones?"

"You see, Paul," the teacher explained. "There is a myth that the female praying mantis always kills her lover after sex. But that isn't true. If her lover mounts her very skillfully, she doesn't kill him. But if he is clumsy in his approach, she just turns her long neck around and bites his head off. Then the poor guy functions naturally long enough to impregnate her."

An image quickly floated through Paul's mind. He was thankful that this technique didn't apply to humans. What had happened in his parents' bedroom had seemed ugly enough.

"Does that myth apply to humans at all, Mr. Jones?" he asked.

"It certainly does, Paul," Mark Jones answered excitedly, and Paul knew right away that he wasn't going to have to ask any more questions. His teacher liked nothing more than an eager student.

"Take your right hand, extend it straight out in front of you and raise it in the air," he directed. Paul did as he was told.

"Now, suppose I were to ask you right now to raise your penis." Paul gulped and his face turned several shades of red, but Mr. Jones only smiled calmly, "Don't worry, Paul. It was only a hypothetical question." Paul relaxed just a little. "You see, sex is not controlled by the voluntary nervous system the way your arm is. It's controlled by the autonomic nervous system— like your heart is. The autonomic is divided into two parts-the sympathetic and parasympathetic systems. The sympathetic controls our fight or flight response. If a bear were all of a sudden to come running from the woods, your body would have to prepare to deal with the threat. But once the threat is over your parasympathetic helps you to relax. It is sometimes referred to as 'feed and breed' because of its role in digestion and sex.

Furthermore, though both the sympathetic and parasympathic play a role it is more controlled by the parasympathetic part of the autonomic nervous system that is also called the 'relaxation response.' So, if sex is going to work, it's important that a person not feel pressured to perform. People can't will themselves to have sex. They have to get their heads out of the way and let their bodies respond."

"And if a person was used to using alcohol or some other substance to relax and then stopped using that substance," Paul asked excitedly, "it could cause him problems sexually?" He was now fascinated by the discussion and momentarily forgot his self-consciousness.

"That is a very good question, Paul," Mr. Jones said with pride. "Yes, it certainly could cause him problems."

Paul was so impressed with his teacher's knowledge and the calm manner in which he discussed such a difficult subject that he just had to ask another question that had been bothering him.

"Mr. Jones, the word around school is that you're not married and that you don't date. How can you know all this if you don't apply it?"

Mr. Jones laughed. "Well, I've never been lucky enough to date a praying mantis, but I do know that this is what the whole thing is about, Paul: you can't make love with your head.

That's the part the female bites off. You have got to make love with your heart." Suddenly, Paul knew that if he could somehow tell his dad about the praying mantises it would make a difference. But how? He couldn't just walk up to his dad and say, "Listen Dad, I know you're having sexual problems and I can help."

Mark Jones stood up and yawned. "Most of the boats seem settled in for the night and the loons seem to be doing the same, Paul. I think I'll knock off. Do you want a ride home?"

"No thanks, Mr. Jones," Paul answered. "I think I'll stay here for a while and then run home. You know, Sally and I have been running every morning and I'm actually beginning to enjoy it. Of course, I'd never tell her that. She thinks I'm doing her this incredible favor and I want to be able to take advantage of that at some point."

The teacher laughed. "Okay, Paul. Will you be by here tomorrow?"

"You bet!" Paul answered.

It was late afternoon, and Paul waited and listened to the loon's wail a few more times. To Paul, the beauty of that sound made taking all the ridicule worthwhile. Then he jogged home.

On the way he thought some more about how he could share what he learned with his father. This was what he had come to like about running: it gave him time to think.

As he jogged, he developed a plan.

CHAPTER 9

• • • • • • • • ● ● ● ⬤ ● ● ● ● • • • • •

WHEN PAUL ARRIVED HOME, DINNER was just about ready. Unlike the other night, everyone was at the table. Hank and Molly were busy arguing, but this time not with each other. They were trying to convince Sally that she should eat with the family now that the track season was over. She finally agreed, but Paul noticed she spent most of her time pushing the food around her plate. The others seemed preoccupied with their own plates, however, and the family ate in silence.

The Brandts had probably always been a family that concentrated more on eating than talking. During the years of Hank's drinking, everyone ate with one eye on the door, wondering when and in what condition he'd come home.

But tonight it was not just the tension in his family that was obvious to Paul. It was the distance between each of them.

He waited until dinner was nearly finished. His mother and father were sipping their coffee and Ryan had just taken his last swallow of milk. "Mr. Jones taught me about sex today,"

Paul said matter-of-factly.

It was probably the absurdity of it that got to all of them. Here they were, in their deadliest, coldest silence, and timid Paul brought up the biggest taboo subject of all. Ryan sprayed his milk across the table. Molly spilled most of her coffee trying to place the cup calmly in her saucer. Sally started giggling uncontrollably, and Bobbie immediately focused all of her attention on the spills. She got up from the table and called Ryan a pig, then went to the kitchen sink for a rag and began furiously moving dishes and wiping up milk and coffee wherever she could find it. Perhaps the strangest reaction came from Hank. He raised his hand in the air to try to quiet the bedlam and with a smile that carried some relief he said to Paul, "What did he teach you?"

As soon as Paul started to talk, however, everyone else in the family started to talk at the same time. Hank again raised his hand, but this time lowered it with more authority. "Quiet!" he said calmly. "What's the matter with you people? Aren't we grown up enough to have a discussion on this subject without mass hysteria? Now, I want to hear what Paul has to say." The kitchen again grew quiet—not so much from tension now as from shock and amazement at both Paul and Hank.

Everyone's amazement grew as Paul made his presentation.

To his recollection, Paul had never before had the attention of his entire family all at once, and to have that attention at the request of his father felt to him like making his debut on Broadway. He proceeded to tell them all about the praying mantises and how the male lives if he mounts his mate the right way. Paul thought at that point he caught his father glancing at his mother, but he wasn't sure.

Everyone howled with laughter when Paul said, "Then the poor guy functions naturally long enough to impregnate her."

Enjoying the laughter coming in his direction for a change, Paul quipped, "Well, you get the point." Next, Paul used Mark Jones's example about raising somebody's right arm and he used his father to demonstrate.

When he then said to his father, "Now suppose I were to ask you to get an erection," bedlam returned. "Oh my God!" Sally shrieked.

Ryan was holding his sides and rocking back and forth, with short bursts of laughter erupting before he contained himself again. Molly simply sat with her mouth open and Bobbie started cleaning again. Hank was too shocked to establish order right away. So Paul said, "Relax guys! It's just a hypothetical question," and went straight into his discussion of the nervous system.

Paul left out the part about Mr. Jones and his dating life because he thought that was something his teacher had told him in confidence. He also knew that if Ryan and Sally heard that part of the story, it would be all over the school system by Monday morning. So he ended with, "And Mr. Jones says that's why you have to make love with your heart, rather than your head."

Sally finally got herself together enough to make a joke.

"That was great, Paul," she said. "What will tomorrow's lecture be on—sex and the single mosquito?"

Everyone laughed, but they applauded Paul at the same time.

Paul acknowledged the applause. "Thank you," he said.

"Now may I be excused? I have to go to the bathroom." As he ran up the stairs, he heard them all laughing and commenting on what he had said.

When Paul reached the bathroom, he had a queasy feeling in his stomach. He realized that he was just excited . . . and proud.

Pride was a new feeling for Paul. He decided that he liked it.

Paul spent most of the rest of the night in his room.

He had had all the interpersonal interaction he thought he could handle for one day. As he lay quietly in his bed, he heard someone enter the bathroom and then vomit. I guess I'm not the only one whose stomach is upset, he thought. A few moments later, Sally stuck her head in the door. "Going running in the morning, Paul? We've got a lot to talk about," she said with a devilish grin.

Paul had to work hard to get the pained "I hate running" expression on his face. "I guess so," he said, sounding burdened.

"Hey, are you okay?" he asked.

"Sure," she replied with a surprised look on her face.

Next Bobbie looked in. "Is that really true about the praying mantis?" she asked.

"I guess so," he answered.

Bobbie looked a little confused herself and closed the door quickly.

Last came Ryan. He stuck his head in the door and in a deadly serious voice said, "Now suppose I ask you to have an erection?" Ryan didn't wait for a reply. Paul could hear peals of laughter as Ryan retreated down the hall.

Paul pretended to be asleep when Ryan came to bed so he could hear what was going on in his parents' room. Ryan was quickly in bed and the lights were off. The room was quiet and Paul listened intently.

Then from the dark corner over by the window came Ryan's voice. "Now suppose I ask you to have an erection?"

The last part of the sentence was hard to understand because Ryan was laughing so hard. Paul felt on the floor for a shoe. He found one and threw it. It hit Ryan as Paul had hoped, but it only encouraged his brother all the more.

"Now suppose . . ." More laughter.

To heck with it, Paul thought. It's up to them now. I've done what I can. Soon he heard his dad snoring. He thought about what Mr. Jones had said: "Knowing is not enough; you have to make love with your heart." Perhaps the heart takes its time, Paul thought as he drifted off to sleep.

After that night, the dinner table at the Brandt house seemed a lot less tense. There was a lot more laughing, and people began to bring up all kinds of issues and feelings. One night Molly commented on the change.

"Heck, Mom," Ryan said. "After Paul's lecture on sex, what could anyone else do or say that would shock this family?" They all laughed, including Paul.

CHAPTER **10**

· · · · · ● ● ● ● ● ● ● ● ● ● ● ● ● ● · · · ·

IN SPITE OF PAUL'S NEW-FOUND interpersonal success, he still liked his solitude. It was more than the loons and nesting site that kept Paul on the other side of the lake and away from the public beach that summer. Paul enjoyed being alone. Though the bottom of the lake on that side was mucky and brown, Paul still preferred to swim there by himself, away from the clean and sandy but crowded public beach. He didn't like sunning himself anyway, and his thin, pre-pubescent body was certainly nothing to show off. Besides, the swampy part of the lake provided many more bugs, frogs and pollywogs to study.

Mark Jones kept a dinghy with a small outboard motor on it near the nesting site. He didn't mind if Paul took it out now and then. The two loners were becoming good friends. In spite of the fact that the loons stayed and the female laid two eggs this time, the other Loonies had lost interest, so Paul was often at the site alone.

So Paul was surprised when Zack Pierce showed up one afternoon.

It seemed to Paul that with each passing day Zack became more handsome. His now dark brown body stood in stark contrast to his blond hair bleached lighter by the sun. His light blue eyes seemed to gaze from deep behind his tanned face.

But it was the person behind the face that was most attractive to Paul. It's been said that God gives alcoholism to those He wants to draw closer to, and it was easy to see why God would want to be closer to Zack. He was kind and gentle and wasn't afraid to show it, even when he was surrounded by his athlete friends. He was wise for a young person, and yet humble. Zack would talk to anyone without putting on an air of being better than his listener.

Zack had grown uncomfortable with the drinking and smoking going on at Roper's, so he had decided to take a walk and check out Paul and the loons. He had taken the path that led through the woods around the lake to the loon nesting site.

Sitting quietly underneath a shade tree, Paul was watching a bass jump for mayflies. He was startled when Zack walked up behind him. "Hi!" Zack said rather softly, but loud enough to make Paul jump higher than the bass.

"Sorry, Paul, I didn't mean to startle you," Zack apologized.

"I thought your specialty was scaring loons," Paul said, embarrassed by his reaction.

"Paul, I wasn't even here that day," Zack said evenly. "And I'm sorry it happened. I like listening to the birds at night too."

Paul's mood changed when he heard Zack was also an admirer of the loons. "I can never decide if I like the yodel or the wail the best," Paul said enthusiastically.

"What's the difference?" Zack asked.

"The wail is shorter, and it's for calling its mate. The yodel is a long series of calls, and it's used when the loon's territory is invaded," Paul answered.

"How'd you get here, anyway?" Paul asked suddenly, realizing Zack didn't totally share his passion for loons.

"I was just walking around the lake," Zack said.

"What, are you bored with drinking and smoking at Roper's?" Paul said sarcastically.

"Drinking? Smoking?" Zack said, trying to looked shocked.

"You know, Zack, your friends may consider me a geek, but I'm not stupid," Paul countered.

"Well, if you're so smart you ought to know I'm recovering and don't do that stuff anymore," Zack replied strongly.

"Oh, yeah, I forgot," said Paul, apologetically. "Sorry."

"It's okay," Zack said. "In a way, I'm glad people forget. I guess that means you don't see me as some sort of freak."

"Are you kidding?" Paul exclaimed. "You're the only one of my brother's friends that I like, and that's because you don't treat me like *I'm* a freak."

"Thanks, Paul. You're a good kid and I like you too," Zack answered sincerely.

"Now that that's out of the way, how are you doing with girls this summer?" Paul asked, trying to change the subject and sound like one of the guys in the locker room.

"Hold on there, young one. Just because I like you doesn't mean I'm ready to share my life history with you," Zack said somewhat playfully.

"I'm sorry," Paul responded. "It's just that Mr. Jones and I were talking a few days ago about . . ."

"Oh, yeah, Ryan told me about the famous praying mantis dinner conversation," Zack said with a laugh. "Well, I date a little bit, but my sponsor suggested I make recovery my number one priority for a while longer. So I don't have a lot of experiences I can share with you. No girl has bit my head off yet if that's what you're wondering."

The two boys laughed. Then they sat for a long time watching the fish and the birds. It was getting later in the afternoon and the activity on the lake was beginning to die down.

"I think I'll swim back to Roper's now," Zack said.

Paul looked at him in disbelief. "You sure you weren't smoking some of that weed before you left?" he protested. "That swim across to Roper's is at least a mile, and those people out there on those power boats aren't that observant—even when they're sober."

"We swim farther than that in practice, Paul, and the boats aren't allowed to come closer than one hundred feet to the shore," Zack replied as he started to wade into the water.

"Well, how about if I ride alongside you in the dinghy?" Paul offered.

"No, that's okay," Zack assured Paul. "You've got the loons to protect and, besides, I've done this hundreds of times."

With powerful strokes, Zack was well on his way back to Roper's within minutes. Paul watched him swim. Zack had always been friendly to him. Maybe it was his good looks and athletic ability that gave Zack the confidence he needed to be friendly with someone like Paul who wasn't "cool." Paul marvelled at the speed with which he moved through the water. His admiration turned to horror, however, when he saw Roper's boat, along with the "tubers" he was pulling, heading at full speed in Zack's direction.

Tubing is like water-skiing, except the "tubers" are pulled by ropes behind a powerboat on large inner tubes, usually truck or tractor tubes. It isn't as challenging as water skiing, because it is easier to stay on. Easier, that is, unless whoever is driving the boat goes very fast and makes sharp turns, whipping the tubes with centrifugal force out over the wake of the boat. Tubing is probably dangerous under the best of conditions, but this was near dusk and these kids had obviously been drinking.

Roper delighted in his ability to lose anyone off a tube within a few minutes and enjoyed watching their bodies turn over several times on top of the water before sinking. At the moment, Ryan and Steve were on the tubes, with Roper driving. Mike, another friend, was supposed to be watching the tubers in case one fell, while the driver watched for other boats.

Both Mike and Roper, however, were watching the boys being whipped around turn after turn. As the boat gradually headed in Zack's direction, Paul decided to follow Zack in the dinghy and ride next to him in spite of Zack's earlier refusal.

The small motor on the dinghy propelled Paul slowly through the water. He had a sick feeling inside. He tried logically to convince himself that the chances of the swimmer and the boat being at the same place at the same time were remote, but his feeling of doom didn't subside. Paul wished that Zack would swim slower or that the dinghy would move faster or that Roper would turn around and look where he was going.

Paul was gaining on Zack, but not as rapidly as Roper was.

Even with the turns and zig-zags Roper made as he tried his best to get Ryan and Steve off the tubes, the powerful boat moved steadily in Zack's direction. Paul tried waving his arms, to no avail. Even if Roper were looking at him, which he wasn't, he would have probably thought Paul was trying to wave him away from the nesting site. In the water, Zack wasn't wearing goggles and couldn't possibly see the boat coming towards him.

The final moments all seemed to happen in slow motion to Paul: the speedboat full of partying and ignorant bliss;

Zack's relaxed, powerful, confident strokes; and Paul's panic and screams, drowned by the motors. The collision seemed imminent. Paul hoped that Zack would hear Roper's boat coming close and dive under the water. Just as the boat was about to hit him, Zack did look up and dive, but Paul wasn't sure that Zack had time to avoid the prop. Roper's boat sped blissfully past and away from Zack, unaware of the possible collision. Paul, his heart in his throat, begged his tiny engine to speed up. He kept hoping to see Zack's head bob out of the water any second. Instead, he saw a crimson slick on the water, which confirmed his worst fears.

Just as Paul arrived at the spot, Zack's pale face emerged from the pool of reddening water. Paul struggled to pull the boy into the dinghy, and he nearly passed out when he saw Zack's ankle and foot. Zack seemed to be in shock, but Paul kept talking to him as he wrapped his t-shirt around the wound.

On the next turn of Roper's boat, Ryan saw Paul pulling Zack into the dinghy. He tried to wave to get Roper's and Mike's attention, but as soon as he did he flew from the tube.

The two laughed and circled to pick him up.

"I knew I'd get you off. You owe me five bucks," Roper shouted with pride in his voice.

Ryan screamed to Roper, "Zack's hurt! Get us in the boat."

Once Ryan and Steve were back in the boat, Roper turned around and sped up beside Paul.

"Killing loons wasn't enough for you?" Paul cried as the boat came within shouting distance. When the older boys saw Zack's injuries, they transferred him into Roper's boat and quickly took off, leaving Paul behind in the dinghy, totally ignored.

The teenagers were terrified. Would their friend be all right? And what were they going to tell the authorities about how the accident happened? While driving Zack to the hospital, they agreed on a story. Roper suggested they say they were going slowly and the boat was riding high in the front, so they didn't see Zack. They all also agreed to insist that Zack had wandered too far out from shore.

Zack, who was in great pain and kept going in and out of consciousness, agreed to the story, as long as Roper's insurance would cover all the damages. The boys all promised they would say nothing about drinking or drugging and, if asked, would deny it.

"What about Paul?" Roper asked. "Will he go along with the story? Do you think he knows we were drinking?"

"I don't know," Ryan said. "He's pretty mad at us about the loon thing. I don't think I can convince him to keep quiet about this."

"I'll talk to Paul," Roper said, sounding mean.

"Don't hurt him," Ryan growled.

"Hey, do you want your old man to find out you were drinking?" Roper yelled. "I'm trying to save your butt." Ryan was silent.

As soon as Roper could slip out of the hospital emergency room without being noticed, he left. On the way out, he saw Paul, who was just arriving on his bike from the lake.

"Hey, Paul! Wait up," Roper called.

Against his better judgment, Paul waited. "What do *you* want?" he asked in the toughest tone he could muster. "I just want to say thanks," Roper said, sounding kind.

"You really saved my hide."

"I didn't do it for you," Paul asserted in disgust.

"Of course not," said Roper. "You did it to save Zack.

You're a hero. I'll make sure that everyone knows about it," Roper answered, remaining calm.

Paul caught on to the kindness act, which had fooled him at first. "Oh, I get it," he said. "I'm a hero and you're nice to me in return for just a few modifications on the facts, right?" Paul said, his voice rising in anger. "Forget it, Roper, nothing will please me more than getting you and your buddies in trouble.

Maybe your parents will even take away your precious boat."

Roper grabbed Paul by the nape of the neck and dragged him behind the building. "You want to make another tombstone for those two new eggs?" Roper threatened. "And maybe have one made for yourself?"

Few people could intimidate as well as Roper, and Paul was genuinely scared. Roper must have discovered the grave the Loonies had made for the first egg. Several thoughts raced through Paul's mind. Had the boys truly missed seeing Zack merely because they were caught up in having a good time, or was it because alcohol and marijuana had made them oblivious?

Paul didn't mind covering for kids just having fun, but what was the difference between a speedboat on a lake and a car on the highway? Drunk drivers have no business in either place. But what about the loons? They were innocent victims too. Paul couldn't bear to see two more babies die.

161

The combination of fear of Roper and compassion for the loons made his decision for him.

"I'll go along with your lies," Paul said, trying not to sound scared. "But you leave the loons alone!"

A sneer came over Roper's face. "I'll treat them like family," he said sarcastically.

THIS WAS TO BE A family day for the Brandts. First, most of them were going to see Sally run in a race with her summer park district team.

Then, it would be on to Bobbie's graduation ceremonies in the evening. Paul was leaving his room when he noticed Sally pacing back and forth in hers.

"Nervous?" he asked as he stepped inside.

"Yeah," she said, continuing to pace. "And Dad made me eat a sandwich, saying I couldn't run on an empty stomach."

She rolled her eyes and continued. "I hate running on a full stomach." She looked at her profile in the mirror. She seemed disgusted.

"Well, one sandwich won't hurt," Paul reasoned. "By the time your race comes up you'll probably be hungry rather than full. Those meets take forever, and you're in one of the last events. Besides, there's no more time to worry. We have to go."

"You go ahead," Sally said with a smile. "I have to go to the bathroom one more time. Nerves, you know." She patted him on the back as they walked from her bedroom, her mood seemingly improved.

By the time Sally ran to the car where Paul, Ryan and her mother and father were waiting, she seemed exhilarated. It was obvious that cares and worries wouldn't be slowing her down today.

Paul was right when he anticipated the meet being long, but it was worth the wait to see Sally run. As she lined up for the mile race, her body didn't stand out; she was just as thin as the other girls. When the gun sounded, she immediately grabbed the lead. As she pulled away, her strides seemed effortless and natural. By the end of the race, she led by several yards. She crossed the finish line looking as though she had just stepped off a bus. The Brandts all jumped and cheered. Sally looked up at the stands with an embarrassed grin and shook her head, but her pride showed through.

That night at Bobbie's graduation from high school, the family was all there to watch her. Even Scott, who had become more and more withdrawn from the family since the intervention, came home from college for the event. The ceremony seemed long and boring to Paul, and he couldn't wait to get out. On the ride home, Bobbie was crying softly in the back seat and Ryan was teasing her.

"Boy, you can bet I won't cry when I graduate!" he promised.

"You mean if you graduate, don't you son?" Hank quipped.

"Now, can't we be nice to each other on this special night?" Molly said. "We're very proud of you, Bobbie. You did a great job in high school."

"Thanks, Mom," Bobbie said. "I just wish I had started to get involved socially sooner than I did. I feel like I just met most of my friends in the last year, and now we'll all be separating and going to different schools."

Before the intervention with Hank, Bobbie had been so involved in keeping peace in the family that she really hadn't taken time for friends. But since that time, she had started dating a boy named Tom, and they both hung around with the same group of friends. Tom was going to be attending the same college as Scott. In fact, he would be leaving for summer school the following week. His grades in high school had not been the best, and he needed the summer courses to prove his ability to the college.

Bobbie, on the other hand, although she had been the top student in her class, was planning to attend the local community college for at least one year. Molly and Hank had asked her to do that until Scott finished college the following year. They said the reason was financial, but Paul thought it was really because Bobbie helped keep the family stable and they were afraid of losing her presence too soon. He also believed Bobbie wanted to stay at home because she still felt so responsible for the family. But Paul kept all these opinions to himself.

"You know," Hank said later that night as they all sat around the kitchen table eating the cake Molly had made for Bobbie, "A lot has happened in the last year that we have to be thankful for. I got sober, Paul is a hero, Bobbie graduated, Sally's a track star, Scott continues to excel in class and on the football field, Molly was named music director at church, and Ryan got his driver's license and a part-time job. I think it's time that we had a big Brandt family party, like we used to have."

"Oh, Hank. Do you think we're ready for something like that?" Molly asked nervously.

"Molly, it's been a year. We can't hide from alcohol forever.

I know I can't drink, but I don't have to avoid fun, too, do I?"

The children all seconded Hank's idea. Scott promised to come home again for the party. Molly finally relented.

Over the next few days, however, Molly continued to argue with Hank about serving alcohol at the party. Hank insisted it would not bother him and that he would feel funny not having anything to offer his friends. Realizing it was useless to pursue the point, Molly gave in. But as the day of the party grew closer, all of the old tension began to surface between them.

Paul could tell that just having alcohol in the house again made Molly uncomfortable.

The party took place on the following weekend. Pastor Brooks came, and having him there was a great comfort to Molly. Hank's brother, Ken, and his wife, Martha, were also there, as were most of the men who worked with Ken and Hank. Scott was there too, with a girlfriend. He seemed to have a cold, because his nose was running constantly.

He appeared uncomfortable around the other people, and every once in a while he would leave and take a walk. After one of these walks, Paul thought he noticed that Scott and his girlfriend were fighting. Shortly after that, Scott said he wasn't feeling well, and they left.

Bobbie had invited almost her entire high school class, and most of them came. It was obvious she was really enjoying herself, and at one point she went up to her father and gave him a big hug. "Thanks, Daddy! I know you did this for me."

She was crying again, with joy. Hank didn't say anything. He just shook his head, because he knew he would be crying too if he tried to talk.

The party was a wonderful mixture of young and old.

Hank was the perfect host, not pushing alcohol but offering it as an option when people asked for a drink. He also made sure none of Bobbie's or Ryan's friends drank. Paul could see that Molly tried very hard not to watch her husband when he made drinks next to her in the kitchen while she was fixing food. She never mentioned anything to him about the alcohol.

Towards the end of the party, she even let Hank pour her a glass of wine.

As the last people left the party and the family was all helping with the cleanup, everyone seemed relieved— not only because the planning and effort of putting together a large event were over, but also because the party itself had gone well, without any incidents or disagreements. Even cleaning up together was fun. Sally made jokes and Ryan teased Bobbie unmercifully about Tom. They all fell into bed that night, tired from the events of the day.

Everyone, that is, except Paul. Midway through the party, he had walked past the pantry to find his father furtively sipping a drink. It was an alcoholic drink, Paul instinctively knew. In shock, he walked out of the kitchen without Hank noticing him. For the rest of the evening, however, Paul had kept a watchful eye on his dad. As near as he could tell, it was Hank's only slip.

Like everything else Paul was carrying on his frail little shoulders, this was a heavy burden. He slept little that night.

CHAPTER 12

WHEN THEY FIRST STARTED, RUNNING had been drudgery to both Sally and Paul. Sally did it only to lose weight and to have an excuse to be out of the house, and Paul did it only as a favor to Sally.

"You know," Sally said to Paul on one of the first mornings of summer vacation, "I have never been very active, and my weight made it difficult for me to feel good doing physical things. When track season started, I had trouble running around the track once without stopping to rest. I wanted to be able to run with the other kids, so I pushed myself hard and stayed late to run extra laps. By the end of the season, I could run more than a mile and my times were dropping and I was winning races. Now I'm really getting to the point that I enjoy running. I can't wait for next fall's cross country season."

The two of them looked like a precision drill team as they moved down the road. Their feet landed at the same time, their strides were equal, even their arms moved in unison.

"You don't even have to run with me anymore, Paul," she announced. "I know I'll keep going on my own."

"I've been playing with you, Sal," Paul confessed. "I enjoy running now, too."

"I thought you did," she said with a smile. "Besides, you're getting good at it. You should go out for cross country in the fall, too."

"No. I want it to be something I do just for myself," Paul said.

"You know, I've lived with you all my life and I still don't understand you," Sally said. "Why don't you want to show off something you're good at?"

"It's not that I don't want to show off," Paul countered.

"It's just that if I do it as a sport I'll have coaches telling me when I have to run and how far, and I'm afraid they'll ruin it for me."

"That makes some sense," Sally said with a laugh. "But you're still weird."

Paul lightly punched her on the arm. They ran for a while in silence.

"Since you're being so free with the compliments," Paul said with a smile, "I can tell that you really have lost weight.

How much have you lost since we started running?"

"I don't know," Sally said quickly, "I'm afraid to step on the scale because I'm still so fat."

Paul looked at her with curiosity. "I don't think you're fat at all anymore," he said. "As a matter of fact, you need to go back to eating regularly. You probably will keep losing weight just because you run so much."

"Well, maybe you're right," Sally replied, "but don't start bugging me like Mom and Dad, okay?"

"Okay," Paul promised.

At the beginning of summer, they had made an agreement to get up and run early every morning. That way, they could run when it was cool. The two youngsters had reached, by now, the point where they felt they could run forever. They would leave the house just after sunrise and run toward the lake, where they would watch the mist rising off the water as they ran in the coolness among the trees. Paul would stop and check on the loons.

After running for several minutes without stopping, they felt as if their legs were no longer attached to their bodies. They moved effortlessly, and their minds were free to wander. Brother and sister could think or talk about things or just watch the world go by as it gradually woke from its slumber. Occasionally, on warmer mornings, they'd wear swimming suits under their shorts and take a dip in the lake before running back home.

This particular morning, Paul watched as Sally poured herself some cereal. He was pleased to see her eat a few bites, but then she poured most of it down the sink. She spread bread crumbs on a plate to make it look as if she had eaten more than she really had. Sally had really become an expert at moving food around so it appeared as if she had eaten.

Hank and Molly walked in just as Sally was leaving the kitchen. She greeted them cheerfully, giving each a kiss on the cheek.

"Oh, are we in one of our friendly moods today?" her mother asked.

"Aren't I always?" Sally answered, stopping dead in her tracks as if she had just been caught stealing from the cookie jar.

"No, you're not," Hank said, chiming in on the conversation.

"You know, Sally, I never thought I of all people would say this to one of my kids, but don't you think you're overdoing this exercise bit a little?"

"You're right, Dad; this is a shock," Sally said, trying to maintain a playful air. "You've always pushed us kids to be in sports and do our best. You've always seemed disappointed that no one has followed in Scott's jock footsteps."

"I know," Hank replied slowly, "but I think you're losing too much weight. And you seem so tired and moody."

"All that didn't seem to bother you when I was coming in first at the meets you came to this spring," Sally snapped, finally raising her voice.

Hank sighed in desperation. "I'm proud of what you've accomplished, Sally, but your health is more important to me than all your victories combined," he said, trying to remain calm.

"I wonder if you'd say that if I were a boy?" Sally yelled.

"Paul runs every day and you don't stop him."

"Paul runs once in the morning and he's not losing weight. Plus, he eats a lot more than you do," Molly retorted.

"I don't understand," Sally screamed. "When I finally do something I think will please you, you get mad at me for doing it. I just can't win in this family."

"Okay, I've had it," Hank shouted back. "I don't want you running any more before dinner, when you will sit down with the family and eat. Molly, you sit down with her now and make sure she eats a decent breakfast," Hank said as he stormed out of the house.

"I ate already," Sally objected, calling after him.

"I know how you ate," her father yelled back.

Sally sat down at the table and slowly ate cereal and a piece of toast. Paul left the kitchen as quickly and as quietly as he could, but Molly sat with her daughter long after she had finished her own breakfast.

"What's wrong with you, Sally?" Molly finally asked. "You used to be so cheerful and ready with a joke, but now you seem almost depressed much of the time."

"Running raises your sugar level and you don't feel hungry right afterwards, Mom," Sally explained. "If I weren't forced to sit here now after coming home from running I would eat better later and I wouldn't be so crabby."

"Okay," Molly said logically. "Then maybe you'll be hungry by dinner if you don't run any more today."

Sally left the table in tears and went to her room. Paul heard her and went to see how she was doing. When he poked his head into the room, Sally was looking at herself in the mirror. "I dread the thought of having to eat dinner, especially if I didn't earn it with a run," she told Paul.

"Sally, you're not fat anymore," Paul tried to reason with her. "With all the exercise you're getting, you don't have to worry about your weight."

Her mood seemed to lighten. "I guess you're right," she said as she moved past him toward the door. "Now if you'll excuse me, I have to go to the bathroom."

Paul knew his sister well, and it seemed to him that recently he could change her mind with only a few words. Maybe he wasn't changing her mind at all. After each discussion, she seemed to cheer up as she headed for the bathroom.

This time Paul listened closely and heard her throw up.

Paul waited outside the bathroom door. When Sally opened the door and saw Paul there, she knew she had been heard. "Don't you dare say a word," she snarled at Paul.

Another secret, Paul thought.

After that, Paul and Sally ran separately.

CHAPTER **13**

Pastor Brooks had called Molly several times during the week before reaching her. "Where have you been?" he asked, sounding slightly perturbed.

"Oh, grocery shopping, clothes shopping, running kids around—you know how it is."

"Yes, I guess I do," he said vaguely. "Listen, I'd like you to do me a favor, Molly. I'd like you to bring your whole family to church this weekend. Do you think they would come?"

"I'm sure they'd come. What's the occasion?" she asked suspiciously.

There was a long pause at the other end of the line. "I'd rather just explain it to you at church, if that's all right," he said.

"Sure," Molly replied. She hung up the phone. What was that all about, she wondered.

Molly told the family that night about Pastor Brooks' request, and they all agreed to go to the first service the next Sunday.

When they arrived at the church, Molly started to open the organ and found a note addressed to her on the music stand. She opened it quickly, thinking it had something to do with the music the pastor wanted her to play that day. She froze as she read the short note.

"Molly, I will be announcing today that I'm being transferred. I wanted you to know first." It was signed: "Love, John Brooks."

Molly played mechanically through the early parts of the service, waiting for the sermon to confirm this harsh reality.

It appeared to Molly that Pastor Brooks' eyes were already watering as he approached the pulpit. As intellectual as ever, he began with a quotation.

"I think it was the famous psychoanalyst Carl Gustav Jung who said, 'Life itself can be seen as a slow progressive disease, from which there is

171

a poor prognosis for recovery.' Before I came to this parish I felt that, in many ways, this statement summed up my philosophy of life."

The congregation stirred visibly. This was not going to be a normal homily.

"I was a part of the living dead until all of you came into my life," he continued. "I used to think I knew life because I was such a good observer. You have all taught me, however, to be a participant, and now I see things very differently. Joshua Krueger was an inspiration to me—as I know he was to many of you. His love of music still rings through this parish each Sunday morning. Since his death, all of you have continued to nurture me and give me life. I feel I've grown up in your loving arms. You have been the compassionate, forgiving family that has helped me to mature, personally and professionally, over the last year."

The stirring had been replaced by absolute silence. Pastor Brooks continued. "One of the things that has helped me to grow has been learning about the philosophies of the various

12-step recovery programs that some of you, my dear friends, are involved in and have shared with me. I've learned much from you about recovery and relapse."

Molly shot a quick glance at Hank, but his eyes were on the floor.

"Recovery is an ongoing, living growth process, and relapse is the absence of recovery," the pastor went on. "There is no such thing as being cured. To avoid relapse, one must actively pursue recovery. Now, this is where my quote from Jung ties in.

You see, it's not just you alcoholic or drug addicted families out there who must embrace recovery. It's all of us. We are either in the process of getting better as a people, or we're getting worse.

We all need to pursue recovery if we want to avoid relapse. We are either growing and embracing life or we are deteriorating and submitting to death."

There was a definite murmuring from the congregation now. They weren't sure they liked what they were going to hear.

"The last years have been the happiest time of my life,"

Pastor Brooks proclaimed in a strong voice. "I could have chosen to stay here in the security of this parish family. But, I've decided that I, too, have to continue changing and that I, too, have to share with others what

I've learned. I've been offered a chance to teach at the seminary. I believe that now I have something to share with prospective clergy that might help them begin 'recovering' earlier than I did. So it is time for me to say thank you and good-bye to you, my family that has nursed me into life. I can say with all sincerity that I love you and I'll miss you. May we all continue to move toward life!"

John Brooks paused to wipe away his tears. Many in the congregation did the same.

"Now, let me hear those wonderful voices that will continue to be a source of inspiration to me for my entire life!" Pastor Brooks concluded. He turned to Molly to signal her to begin the hymn and gave her the kindest smile she could remember since Josh Krueger did the same thing over a year before.

Molly cried on and off through the rest of the service.

They weren't exactly tears of sadness. She felt happy for her friend, although she knew she would miss him fiercely. On the church steps afterwards, she hugged Pastor Brooks. There was little need for words between them. Then the whole family said good-bye. Though the minister had been closest to Molly, he had been a part of all of their lives. When he got to Paul, he said, "I think that, out of your whole family, I identify most with you, Paul. Next to your mother, I will miss you most of all." Somehow, Paul realized that from Pastor Brooks' sermon he had the theme for another dinner lecture.

· · · · · · ● ● ● ● ● ● ● ● ● ● ● ● ● · · · ·

THE INJURY TO ZACK PIERCE was not as serious as the doctors first thought, but it was still a welcome sight when Paul saw him through the binoculars walking toward the loon site. It was an exciting day for Paul, because the two baby loons had just hatched. After their parents had cleaned them up, they looked like two little balls of fluff. To Paul, they were the cutest things he had ever laid eyes on.

"Next to those two loon babies, seeing you walking normally is the best thing I've seen in a long time," Paul said to Zack as he arrived at the site.

"You mean they've hatched?" Zack asked, genuinely excited. "Can I see?" He grabbed the binoculars from Paul and put them up to his eyes. The cord, however, was still around Paul's neck. Zack didn't seem to notice Paul's discomfort as he peered at the two babies.

"Wow, they're brown!" Zack exclaimed. "I never expected them to be brown."

Paul tapped the taller boy on the shoulder, but Zack kept looking and talking. "Zack," Paul finally said. "The cord!"

Zack finally put down the binoculars and Paul took a deep breath. Zack looked down at the cord attached to the binoculars, and then at Paul's face as it gradually changed from purple to pink. First he started to laugh, and then he apologized. "Oh, Paul, I'm sorry," he said, still laughing a little.

"Here you save my life, and this is how I treat you."

"Well, I don't think I saved your life. You only ended up with some stitches. Still, I do wish you wouldn't hang me with my own binoculars," Paul stammered.

"Paul," Zack said in a much more agitated voice. "You did save my life. True, I just had some stitches, but there were a lot of stitches. And when you pulled me out of that water I was in shock. I would have drowned. Paul, those others would never have noticed me if you hadn't been there.

So don't minimize what you did. You're the reason I'm alive today and I'm here right now to thank you for that." Zack put his arm around Paul.

"Thank you."

Paul rarely looked people in the eye, but he looked right at Zack and said, "You're welcome."

Then after a pause, Paul asked, "But how come you sound mad at me?"

"I'm not mad at you for saving my life, Paul. I'm mad at you for not giving yourself the credit you deserve," Zack said in a calmer tone. "But I mean it. Thank you."

Paul waved his hand and smiled. "It was nothing." Zack put his fist to Paul's chin, but he was smiling. "Could I look at the babies again?" he asked. "This time I'll do it without the cord wrapped around your neck."

"Sure," Paul said, carefully removing the cord and handing him the binoculars.

As he looked at the babies, Zack's expression changed from excited to serious. "What' s the matter?"

Paul asked.

"There's another reason I came here, Paul, and it's not anywhere near as pleasant," Zack said in a somber tone.

"What's the matter?" Paul asked.

"I have remembered what actually happened the day you saved me, and I've decided to tell people about it. I have to tell my parents and your parents, for instance, and if I do that I know they'll tell Roper's parents."

Paul was terrified of the implications of Zack's announcement. "But if Roper gets in trouble, even if I'm not the one who told, he'll kill these babies for sure, just for spite,"

Paul blurted out. "Is your honesty worth those babies dying?"

"I know," Zack replied gently. "Ryan told me that Roper threatened you with killing the loons if you talked. That's why I got sad looking at them just now," Zack said.

"Then why would you tell, knowing that would happen?"

Paul asked, wishing the tears weren't welling up in his eyes.

"Paul, this life that you saved won't be worth much to me if I go back to drinking and using drugs, and right now the only way that I can see to avoid that is to follow my 12-step program. The cornerstone to that program is honesty. If I don't tell what truly happened that day I will not only be dishonest, I will be enabling those guys to keep doing the kinds of things they are doing."

Just then, Roper's boat zoomed by in the middle of the lake.

"I know that he's out there right now and that he's been drinking. If I keep quiet, I may save the loons but people may die. I can't live with that responsibility and stay sober. I'm truly sorry, Paul, but I have to tell. And if it means my camping out here the rest of the summer to try to save these little birds, I'll do it. But I've got to tell."

"It doesn't matter if you camp out here. We're no match for Roper's boat," Paul said, the tears now streaming down his face.

"Maybe if Roper's parents find out what happened, they'll take his boat away," Zack countered.

"Yeah," Paul said, "and then he'll really be mad."

"There's an expression in the program, 'first things first'," said Zack. "I've got to tell the truth first, and then I'll do what I can to help out with Roper. Do you understand, Paul?"

Paul again looked in Zack's eyes. He could see that Zack really was concerned about what Paul thought. "I understand,"

Paul said simply.

Then Paul had an idea. It was so perfect that he got very excited.

"Zack, since you want to tell my parents, how about if we do it together?" he suggested. "Sure, but why?" Zack asked, curious at what his little friend was cooking up.

"Well, if Ryan's going to get confronted about the accident, then there are a few other things that ought to be mentioned.

Ryan shouldn't be the only one in the family that gets heat for covering things up. Your being there would give me the courage to do some confronting of my own. And besides, some honesty might help my recovery too," Paul said with a faraway look.

Zack looked at Paul strangely, but he quickly agreed. The two of them planned how they would do it. They finally decided to write letters, like people do during formal interventions.

They felt that way they'd have a better chance of getting out exactly what they wanted to say, and the family would be more likely to hear them all the way through.

Paul and Zack each wrote his letter that night, and they met at the loon site the next day to review them with one another. Zack was a frequent dinner guest at the Brandt's anyway, so it was easy to arrange to have him over for dinner that night. As they prepared, Paul was happy to observe he wasn't the only one who was nervous.

CHAPTER **15**

• • • • • • • • • • ● • • • • • • • • • •

PAUL AND ZACK WERE QUIET at the Brandt dinner table that night, but no one seemed to notice. There was plenty of talking and everyone seemed relaxed. One of the reasons that Paul hated doing this confrontation was that the people in his family were just getting comfortable with each other again. Everyone was just finishing up dinner when Zack and Paul pulled out their letters.

"We have a few things to say to all of you. Will you hear us out?" Zack asked calmly.

The room suddenly got very quiet. "Of course we'll listen,"

Hank said. They had all been through Hank's intervention and guessed that something serious was happening.

Zack went first:

Dear Ryan,

You have been my best friend since grade school. I truly value our friendship and the thought of losing it scares me to death, but we have little if we don't have honesty within that friendship. I can no longer live with continuing a lie about what truly happened the day I was hurt and what continues happening since then. I am afraid when you and Roper and your other friends drink and smoke and then go boating and skiing with his boat. I was not seriously hurt, but someone else—possibly you—may be someday, and I couldn't live with myself if I stood by and let that happen.

I care about you, Ryan, and that's why I'm saying this now. I don't want to get you in trouble, but I want what is going on to stop. I'm saying this in front of your parents because I don't believe either you or I can stop it on our own.

Love, Zack

Ryan immediately looked at his father with fear in his eyes. He could see the anger building in Hank's face.

Before either of them had a chance to speak, however, Zack spoke up again. "Paul has a few things he'd like to say before you react to this," he said. "Since without him I don't believe I would be alive today, I wish you'd listen to him." The room again got very quiet.

Paul had heard little of what Zack said. He had read a book recently called *Tales of the Loon*. It said that in Native American mythology warriors would go to the loon when they needed strength. They would hang on to the loon's wings as the loon plunged deep into the water.

As he waited for Zack to finish, Paul too went to his brother, the loon, for strength. He could feel himself diving with the bird, and he hoped that when they reached the surface he would be strong enough to do what he had to do.

He heard Zack finishing just as he felt himself break out of the water. He started his own letter:

Dear Family,

A couple of weeks ago, we all went to church and heard Pastor Brooks talk about recovery and relapse. I'd like to start by saying I'm happy for the recovery of this family, but I'm also aware of all the ways we are relapsing, and I don't think we're being honest about those things. Zack says that honesty is the cornerstone to recovery. So I've decided that it's time I got honest.

Dad, I'm proud of the effort you have been putting into your recovery. That is why when I saw you take a sip of alcohol at the party we had recently, it scared me . . .

"I knew we shouldn't have had alcohol," Molly shouted.

Hank looked confused, angry and embarrassed all at the same time.

"Mrs. Brandt," Zack interrupted. "Paul isn't finished and you promised you'd hear us out."

Molly became silent.

One by one, Paul named each of the family's secrets:

Sally, I love you more than as a sister. You've been my best friend since you were born. I hate the distance that has come between us. But I can't sit by and watch you starve yourself. You throw up when Dad makes you eat, and you don't have a big meal at lunch like you say you do.

We all know Scott is using cocaine, and, Bobbie, you spend time with him every weekend now and haven't said a thing about it. Besides, I'd like to see you get your chance at going away to college yourself but I believe you won't because you don't think we can get along without you.

Mom is the only one of us that goes to Al-Anon meetings, even though we should all be going. And, Mom, maybe we would go if you would act like they are doing you any good. But after a year, you're still trying to control Dad's drinking.

I love you all, but we all have to get more help.

Love, Paul

The room was absolutely still as Paul finished his letter and then dived for the second time with the loon. Suddenly, everyone wanted to talk. Hank got his out first.

"I just took one sip to see if I could," he protested. "It' s not like I relapsed."

"I told you we shouldn't have had booze in the house!"

Molly screamed again.

Zack intervened. "You're right, Mr. Brandt. That wasn't the relapse." For the first time anyone in the family could remember, Zack sounded aggravated with them. "The relapse started long before that. It probably started with your paying less attention at meetings, then attending fewer meetings.

It started with your listening less and talking less with your sponsor. It started when you began feeling angry, lonely, and even depressed without doing anything about it.

Hank started to react, but Zack continued. "And it didn't just start with you. It's not only your relapse, it's the whole family's relapse."

"And now, I'll say something else I probably shouldn't say,"

Zack concluded. "I've been a part of this family since I was little. I love every one of you. Each of you is a delightful person with special talents. What is so very sad is that not one of you believes in yourself or in each other. Now, you can let what Paul and I just shared destroy you or help you recover."

Zack's speech seemed to change the tone of the entire gathering. For the first time since the intervention, Hank started to cry. He didn't sob, but tears ran down his face as he turned to Molly. Hank's mere look could make anyone in the family feel as small as an ant or as tall as a building, but nothing had more power than his tears. Molly grabbed his hands.

"Molly, this isn't what we want," he said. "I feel like I'm back on the bottom again and I need your help to put the pieces back together. I need to know you still love me. In time, I hope you'll trust me again too, but you have to let me make alcohol my problem."

"Why does it always take a crisis?" Molly cried softly. "I'm sorry I've been so caught up in alcohol, Hank. I've been focused on it and oblivious to you, as strange as that may sound. You need to know that I'm committed to you and our family and that I do love you. It's time for me to focus on people again."

"Thanks for that, Molly," Hank said with genuine relief.

"I believe we can make it if you and I are pulling in the same direction, but I think we need more help. How do we get it?"

The family continued talking. Sally protested that she didn't have a problem. Bobbie admitted that she thought Scott had a drug problem, but she denied vehemently that she was afraid to leave home. With a good deal of parental encouragement, Ryan talked about the parties at Roper's and about the accident with Zack.

Hank finally raised his arm. "Your mother and I need to talk. We have to address these issues one at a time. We'll all meet at breakfast to talk about this further."

Paul and Zack looked at each other. A small smile appeared on both their lips. Zack flashed Paul a "thumbs up" sign just as in the distance a loon gave its crazy call.

PAUL'S PRIMARY CONCERN, AS HE lay in his bed in the dark that night, was the fact that Ryan lay in the bed right next to him, within easy striking distance. He knew by the irritated sighs and the restlessness that Ryan wasn't sleeping. He was afraid to ask Ryan what he was thinking, for fear of what the answer might be. Besides, Paul had done all the initiating he felt capable of for a while.

Suddenly, by the light coming in the window Paul saw Ryan's silhouette sit up. Paul cringed.

"There is a part of me that definitely wants to kick your butt, Paul," Ryan said.

Paul curled up in his bed, waiting for his brother to pounce.

"But you didn't let the family focus just on my problem,"

Ryan continued from his bed, "which definitely would have happened if you hadn't said what you said. I appreciate that.

So I'm going to wait to see what happens to me before I beat the snot out of you."

What a relief! Paul thought, I get to live—at least until tomorrow. Ryan lay back in his bed.

Paul then turned his attention next door. There was a continuous murmuring that Paul couldn't identify. A lot of it sounded angry, but just before he fell asleep he thought he heard a girlish sound that seemed only slightly like his mother's voice.

When he walked into the kitchen the next morning, Paul's suspicions were confirmed. There were his mother and father, hugging and looking at each other in a way they hadn't for a long time.

"Don't let me interrupt," he said with a grin.

His parents immediately opened their arms and invited him into their embrace. Somewhat awkwardly, he joined them.

Being held by the two of them like this made him feel as safe as a baby, at least for the moment. Then Hank sat him down in a kitchen chair and took another across from him while Molly looked on.

"Paul," his dad said quietly. "You know I love sports, and especially football."

Paul nodded his head. Inside he groaned, thinking this was going to be another "Paul, you should be involved in sports" lecture.

"I thought the greatest thrill of my life was to watch your big brother Scott play," Hank said gently. "My favorite part of all was when we were waiting for the first kickoff and all the excitement of the game was in front of me. Then Scott would catch the ball and start running toward the other team. He would hurl himself full speed at the other team running at him full speed. I was so proud of him at that moment. I thought that was the most courageous thing I could ever see my kids do. I guess that's why it's never been a secret that I was disappointed when you and Ryan didn't follow in his footsteps."

Paul started to respond. His worst fears were being confirmed. He was a big disappointment to his father.

Hank interrupted before Paul could say anything. "Wait, Paul, hear me out. But when you did what you did yesterday, I realized that your action—though it will never make a trophy case—is the bravest thing I'll ever see one of my children do."

Paul tried to speak again but his father kept going. "As a matter of fact, Paul, your play last night is in another league from Scott's," Hank said earnestly. "If Scott were hurt being tackled, he would recover. It would only be a physical injury."

"But you risked a kind of injury from which you might never have recovered, Paul," Molly finished. "You ran full speed at the people who loved you and could have hurt you emotionally and spiritually. We're as proud of you as we could ever be of a child."

Paul rubbed the tears from his eyes and gave his mom and dad another hug. This is great, he thought.

Hank addressed the whole family at breakfast. "I guess I have to start with myself first," he said. "What Paul said last night made me realize how scared I am. I say I don't want to drink again—and I believe that! But I have to do my part to make that happen, and I haven't been. I have a new reason to go to meetings now, and I'll be there with a different attitude."

"Today, I'm going to call my sponsor and tell him about my slip at the party," Hank declared. "And I need to get started on that fourth step I've been putting off."

"I'm not as far along as your father," Molly interjected. "I have to work on my first step. But you can bet I'll be doing it."

"Now, as for the rest of you," Hank said firmly. All the children shifted uncomfortably in their chairs. "Ryan, you are grounded for a week, and your mother will be calling the other parents. Our main question is whether you have a serious problem with alcohol and drugs or are just experimenting, so we'll be taking you to the treatment center for an assessment."

"I don't think I've got a problem, but I'll go to talk to someone," Ryan answered quickly, sounding relieved at the relative lightness of the sentence.

"We'll all be there to support you—and also so that you don't minimize what you've done. I know all about doing that,"

Hank said with a rueful smile.

"Sally, you'll have to go for an assessment too," Hank said.

"Why me?" Sally shouted, jumping up. "I don't have a problem. I just wish you'd all leave me alone!"

"Sit down," Molly commanded. "Honey, we care too much about you to take that chance. We'll be with you."

Sally sat sullenly, glaring at Paul.

"We know these are hard things to hear—and hard changes to make," Hank said to his family. "But what Paul and Zack said to us last night was hard for them too. We need to respect their courage and take a look at what they are saying to us. We need to love ourselves as much as they love us."

Everyone looked at Paul, who stared at his cereal.

"But there's one family problem we're not sure how to handle," Hank continued. "We're not sure what to do about Scott. I hate ignoring the problem, but I don't think we can order him to get help. And he has been so distant lately I don't think an intervention by us would have any impact."

Bobbie spoke up for the first time.

"I'm afraid that's true," she said. "I hope I'm not just making excuses for myself for not doing something before, but that's one of the reasons I haven't said anything to him. He's so angry at this family right now that I think anything we did or said right now would only make him angrier."

"There is something we can do that won't antagonize him," said Molly quietly. "We can get better ourselves . . . and pray for him."

Hank took Molly's hand and everyone grabbed the hand of the next person. For the first time in a long time, the Brandt family truly prayed together.

THE FOLLOWING WEEK WAS A busy one for the Brandts. Assessments for both Ryan and Sally took place, and the entire family was involved in each.

The counselors thought that, at the moment at least, Ryan was not addicted to either alcohol or drugs. He had definitely abused them both, however. The counselor suggested that, with their genetic predisposition towards alcoholism, probably none of Hank's children should drink.

Sally, on the other hand, definitely did have an eating disorder. They found an imbalance of salts and potassium in her body serious enough to require two days in the hospital.

The counselor recommended both individual and family counseling. Sally still denied that she had a problem, however, and continued vocally to resist counseling.

Paul was sure that Sally and Ryan now hated him, but he had other things to worry about. Roper's parents had only grounded him for three days, and that sentence was now up.

Today, as Paul kept close watch, the loon babies were getting their first swimming lesson. At first, they rode on their mother's back and she stayed close to the nest, but then she ventured further out.

Roper's grounding apparently had little effect, because he was sitting on his dock drinking beer with a bunch of guys. As soon as he saw the loons, he and his friends boarded his boat and headed for them.

"I'll show that little punk he shouldn't have ruined my summer," Roper declared to his friends as he headed full speed toward the nesting site.

The mother loon and her babies were several feet out from shore when Paul saw Roper's boat heading in their direction.

The mother was in no danger. She could easily dive 200 feet, if need be, to avoid the boat. But the baby loons had not yet learned to swim, much less dive. They would float like corks to be churned by the propeller like eggs in a blender.

Paul moved into action instantly. He had already decided what he would do and he didn't waver now. He had gotten the idea from watching a nature program on how an environmental group saved whales from the whalers' harpoons.

He ran straight to the dinghy. He panicked when two pulls didn't start the small motor. Roper's boat was coming closer to the loons. On the third try, the motor finally caught.

Paul quickly circled the dinghy between Roper and the loons.

When Roper saw Paul, his eyes brightened and he pushed the throttle all the way down, daring Paul to stay in his path.

Paul could feel his heart pounding in his chest as the boat barreled towards him. It now became a battle of nerves.

Zack had stopped at the public beach on his way to the loon site just in time to observe Paul getting into position.

There was no time to swim across the lake, and he knew no one would hear his cries over the roar of the engines.

Zack jumped into his car and headed toward the nesting site. He had to drive around the lake to get there, and he could only imagine what was happening from occasional glimpses through the trees.

Paul's eyes were closed, waiting for impact, when Roper finally turned aside. The wake from the large boat nearly turned the dinghy over. When Paul opened his eyes, he saw the big boat circling for another run at him. He noticed that the loons were safely ashore, and, not wanting to see if Roper would miss again, Paul turned his little boat toward shore. He purposely headed toward a spot away from where the loons had gone, and he reached the sand just as Roper's boat pulled in next to him.

Paul tried to run, but it was useless. Roper grabbed him before he had gotten ten feet. Paul struggled but was ineffective against Roper and his friends.

"You don't look so brave now, you little worm," Roper hissed. "Remember when I told you about that other grave we would have to dig? I'm not going to kill you, though, I've got a better idea." Roper turned to his friends. "Hey, let' s throw him naked on the public beach!"

Somehow Roper knew that Paul despised his skinny body. Paul would skip gym just because he hated taking showers in front of others. The thought of being naked on a beach with people laughing made him sick. Paul also hated being held down. It reminded him of the times his brothers had done that to tease him when he was even smaller. He would sometimes dream of being trapped in a cave-in, and that same feeling of panic overwhelmed him now.

The boys had already pulled off Paul's shirt by the time Zack arrived.

"Leave him alone!" Zack yelled as he ran up.

"Oh, Zack, you've come to save your hero?" Roper mocked.

"You're a little outnumbered, don't you think?" he laughed.

"You nearly killed me once, Roper," Zack said angrily, "I guess you'll get a second shot at it. The first time you had your boat. Now you're with your friends, but this time I'll get in at least one punch and count on the fact that it will land on your face."

"This is going to be even more fun than I thought!" Roper said with satisfaction. "We'll see how high and mighty you are when you and Paul are both naked on the beach. Too bad your friend Ryan isn't here," Roper replied as he and three of his friends left Paul and walked slowly toward Zack and began to circle him. "We could see whose side he would be on."

"With my brother and my best friend," a voice said from the woods. Ryan walked into the clearing with Sally, who had been swimming and had called home from the beach when she first saw Roper heading toward Paul. When Ryan received Sally's call he tried to run immediately from the house, but Molly stopped him. "Where do you think you're going, young man?" she asked.

"Roper's after Paul," was all Ryan needed to say. Molly held out the car keys and told him to hurry.

Meanwhile, Sally had run the distance between the beach and the loon site in record time. She was just picking up a large stick when Ryan arrived. Brother and sister had silently looked at each other and then dashed toward the lake.

"So you're a Loonie now too, Ryan?" Roper said with a laugh. He had six friends with him, so he felt fairly confident.

"A real bird lover. And speaking of birds, here's the whale turned stork," he said to Sally.

Sally glared at Roper and started toward him with the stick, but Ryan held her back.

"No, I don't care much about birds," Ryan said, looking at Paul's frightened eyes. Then his face softened, "But I love my brother and you're not going to hurt him," Ryan said firmly.

"Do you and your big jock friend and your little sister and brother really think you can stop all of us?" Roper said confidently.

"Well, we'll never find out, big shot," Zack said, "because six of you have already left for that boat you like to aim at people."

Roper looked around anxiously to see his friends getting into the boat. "Just wait till you want something from me again," he said pointing at Ryan and starting to back away. Ryan grabbed Paul's torn shirt from Roper's hands and Roper jumped. He then ran toward his boat.

Roper was climbing into the boat when another voice came from the woods. "Just a minute, young man," Mark Jones called as he walked toward Roper.

"What do you want, wimp?" Roper called as he climbed into his boat.

Mr. Jones walked up to Paul. "Are you all right?" he asked.

Paul nodded his head.

"Sorry I haven't been here for a while, but I didn't abandon you or the loons," Mr. Jones said gently. "I've been busy."

The teacher then walked into the water with his shoes and socks still on so he could get just inches from Roper's face.

"I just wanted to let you know, Mr. Roper, that this area is now approved by the State Department of Natural Resources as a wildlife preserve," he said loudly, "and if I see you or your friends over here again, I'll have you arrested. Second, I know a reporter who is doing a story on alcohol abuse and boating and she's very interested in the true story of what happened to Zack. I think publicity might finally get your parents' attention about you. I'm also going to add today's incident to the pot. Now get out of here."

The snarl on Roper's face was replaced by a look of fear.

He started the boat engine and sped off.

Ryan turned to Paul and handed him his shirt. He put his arm around his little brother's bare shoulders, which were suddenly not quite so burdened. "Let's go see those loons you're so crazy about," Ryan said with a big smile. He put his other arm around Zack and said simply, "Thanks."

Sally walked to the other side and added her arm to Paul's shoulders. "Yeah," she said. "Let's get close and see if the chicks follow Paul or their mother."

Everyone, including Mr. Jones, laughed. Paul just smiled.

CHAPTER 18

"LET'S GO, BRANDTS!

It's cold out here," Zack yelled as he ran in place outside their house.

Soon Ryan, Sally, and Paul appeared on the porch in their running gear. The friends all took off for the lake. It was late autumn now, and they had been back in school for a few months. The bond between Ryan and Zack had become stronger, and Ryan no longer was hanging out with Roper and his gang. As a matter of fact, Ryan was trying out for the swim team. He was getting a late start as a senior, but he and Zack were running each morning and swimming in the pool each afternoon. Zack was sure Ryan would at least make some of the relay teams.

This morning, as usual, the two teenagers ran a little faster than Sally and Paul and were soon well ahead of them. They joked and laughed with each other as they pulled away down the road.

Paul and Sally followed. They had begun running together again after the incident with Roper. Sally was still having trouble with her eating disorder, but her parents encouraged her to continue to run and participate in other sports because they knew it was one thing that really helped her feel better about herself. She was eating more regularly, and part of her therapy was to help her mother do the grocery shopping.

Nothing had changed in Scott's life, as far as anyone knew, but the family always included him in the prayer they now shared each night before dinner. Molly told Pastor Brooks in one of their frequent visits that she thought God was the most successful therapist anyway.

One of Paul's biggest surprises had come on one of the last days of summer, when his mother visited him at the loon site.

She brought a lunch for the two of them and stayed most of the day. "I forgot how peaceful nature allows me to be," she said as she sat sunning herself and watching the four loons swim.

Bobbie kept the family informed about Scott after her visits to his college to see her boyfriend, Tom. She was visiting nearly every weekend now and had already applied to attend the same college herself the following semester.

As for Paul, he was still much the same, but he was slowly becoming more outgoing. Sally was still his best friend, and Mr. Jones was still his favorite teacher. One day, Mark Jones brought a date to a junior high basketball game at school. Paul caught his attention as they sat in the stands, then folded his arms like a praying mantis. Mr. Jones laughed and turned to his date.

"I think I just saw a praying mantis in the hall," he said slyly to his woman friend. "Did I ever tell you about their mating practices?"

"Several times," she said with a smile.

Roper never bothered the loons again, but that didn't mean they were out of danger. Because they were hatched so late, there was a chance they wouldn't learn to fly before the lake froze for the long Wisconsin winter. Loons are very heavy birds for their size. That weight is a great help in diving but a liability during takeoffs. And, since they don't nest in trees, the young have to learn the difficult art of taking off from the lake: a long, hard run across the water with wings flapping vigorously before eventual take off.

It had been a long and beautiful fall, but the leaves had now fallen and a skim of ice was appearing on the lake during the long nights. If the young loons couldn't take off soon, the lake would freeze over and they would die.

Paul was nervous as he and Sally approached the lake this morning for fear it had frozen over solid during the cold night.

As they approached the lake, they saw Zack and Ryan jumping up and down and waving their arms. Paul and Sally sprinted to see what the commotion was about. They arrived just in time to see the two young loons, side by side, finish their long runs and clear the water for their first flight.

Paul, Sally, Ryan and Zack hugged one another. The loons might have to stop at several other lakes along their flight south to warmth and safety, but they'd make it now. Paul felt like a proud parent who drops his child off at school for the first time.

He knew that his brother, the loon, would return next spring.

"You know, Paul," said Sally, as they walked home together,

"you've had quite a summer. You've saved two loons and two people. You can be very proud of yourself."

'Two people?" Paul asked, confused.

"Yes. Zack . . . and me," she said. She put her hand on his shoulder. "Thanks, brother," she said sweetly. Then she punched him in the stomach and took off running home.

Paul followed, running like the loons flew. He was aware of his feet touching the ground for a few more steps, but after that he was soaring.

The Importance of Social Workers and Other Allied Disciplines
to be Cross-Trained in Addiction-Related Features
Rob Castillo, *LCSW, CAADC, MISA II*
Associate Professor, ~ Aurora University

The purpose of this brief paper is to advocate for fellow social workers as well as other related disciplines to become properly trained in various aspects of alcohol and other drug addiction (AODA) issues that confront us on a daily basis. It would be difficult to identify an area of social work, (or other social service arenas) that is not potentially impacted by the scourge of addiction.

It will not be the goal of this paper to inundate the reader with a plethora of facts and statistics. Although key statistics will be utilized to stress certain points, the goal is for the reader to gain an increased appreciation for how rampant and unrestrained the problem of AODA has truly become within our society. Ideally at the conclusion of reading this paper, readers will be motivated to pursue, at the very least, ongoing training related to AODA concepts as it pertains to their particular disciplines. Hopefully some readers may chose to go even further and pursue additional education / credentials to add to their current qualifications.

The Drug Abuse Warning Network (DAWN) is a Public Health surveillance system that monitors drug-related hospital emergency departments (EDs) and drug-related deaths investigated by medical examiners (MEs) and coroners which was created and monitored by the Substance Abuse and Mental Health Services Administration (SAMHSA). In 2011, the DAWN report estimated a staggering 2.5 million ED visits which involved medical emergencies related to drug use or misuse. To put these numbers in a more comprehensive perspective, this equals approximately 790 ED visits per 100,000 populous (DAWN, 2011).

DAWN reports that between 2004 and 2011, the number of annual ED visits per year which was attributable to drug misuse has steadily risen each year to a total increase of 52% (2011). The reason this information is so critical is that many times the ED, in their attempt to quickly address the "chief complaint" of the patient, may inadvertently miss an opportunity to intervene with what may actually be the underlying issue of the patient, (AODA).

Triage is an area where nursing and intake staff may be able to begin attempting to tease out potential AODA-related issues. ED social workers and discharge planners are also excellent points of assessment for substance-related concerns.

Social workers are often one of the first service providers to meet with various clients who "walk through the door" (Hall et al., 2000; as cited in Smith, Whitaker, and Weismiller, 2006). The setting could be in an ED as described above, it could be in traditional substance abuse or community mental health agencies, Employee Assistance Programs (EAP) may refer an employee to assess problematic behaviors of an employee, and many clients may be seen within or due to the criminal justice (CJ) system. Children and adolescents who struggle with school are often seen by the school social worker as a "triage" or first line of assessment in dealing with the child's concerns. Many times substance abuse is a part of the underlying issue which brought the child to the attention of the worker in the first place. There could be AODA misuse either within the home; i.e. parental use, or a sibling could be in trouble with substances; or the child him/herself could be using substances for a variety of reasons.

Domestic violence (DV) workers often see the connection between AODA use and offenses. One study found that 92% of the assailants in this particular study reported that they used some form of AODA the day of their arrest (Brookhoff, et al.,1997; as cited in Fisher and Harrisson, 2009). AODA professionals will see that many times both partners in the couple-ship will use substances, which can create a tumultuous relationship.

In 2008, a study came out by Dr. Larry Bennet, in which he studied the link between DV and AODA issues. Bennet cites one study (Fals-Stewart, 2003) which found in their specific sample that DV was eight times more likely to occur on a day the batterer had used alcohol as opposed to a day the batterer was sober.

Many times woman who are involved in DV relationships will find that they also will use various substances themselves. This could be part of the dynamic of their lifestyle or a result of attempting to self-medicate emotional and physical pain. Woman who find they may be struggling with AODA issues may find it is even more difficult to enter treatment, especially if they need residential or Intensive Out-Patient programs. Childcare issues for woman who are the primary care giver is just one of many barriers that make it difficult for women to enter treatment. Other barriers may exist on several levels:

- Intrapersonal: Individual factors including health problems, psychological issues, cognitive functioning, motivational status, treatment readiness, etc.
- Interpersonal: Relational issues including significant relationships, family dynamics, support systems, etc.
- Sociocultural: Social factors including cultural differences; the role of stigma, bias, and racism; societal attitudes; disparity in health services; attitudes of healthcare providers toward women; and others.
- Structural: Program characteristics including treatment policies and procedures, program design, and treatment restrictions.
- Systemic: Larger systems including Federal, State, and local agencies that generate public policies and laws; businesses including health insurance companies; and environmental factors such as the economy. (Substance Abuse and Mental Health Services Administration, 2009, p. 84)

The criminal justice system is definitely an area where AODA issues are prevalent. However, when we discuss crime as it relates to AODA, it is important to understand that there are various levels of relationships between drugs and crime. The following chart was created based on information ascertained from the Bureau of Justice Statistics, (1992; as cited from Zilney, 2011, p. 173).

The Relation Between Drugs and Crime		
Relationship	Definition	Example
Drug-defined crimes	Violation of laws prohibiting or regulating the possession, use, distribution, or manufacture of illegal drugs	Drug possession or use; marijuana cultivation; methamphetamine production; sale of illegal substances
Drug-related crimes	Offenses in which a drug's pharmacologic effects contribute; offenses motivated by the users need for money to support continued use; and offenses connected with drug distribution	Violent behavior resulting from drug effects; stealing to get money to buy drugs; violence against rival drug dealers
Crimes associated with drug use	Drug use and crimes are common aspects of a deviant lifestyle; the likelihood and frequency of involvement in illegal activity is increased because drug users are exposed to situations that encourage crime	A life orientation with emphasis on short-term goals supported by illegal activities; opportunities to offend resulting from contact with offenders and illegal markets; criminal skills learned from other offenders

According to the National Center on Addiction and Substance Abuse (NCASA, 2010), approximately 70 to 85% of the offenders in the United States that have violated drug laws were either under the influence at the time of their arrest, committed the crime to support their drug habit, or had a history of substance abuse.

A common error made in addressing many clients whether in the CJ system or out in the community is the use of the term "rehabilitation". The use of this term tends to indicate we are "re- doing" something that the client once had. For many clients this is an erroneous assumption. Perhaps a better term and approach might be to "habilitate" the client; to help train them with desperately needed skills that for a variety of reasons they just never learned. Examples of this could be job interviewing skills, obtain a GED, and other skills that may be needed. For others it may be more clinical, such as treating unresolved issues other than the addiction. Perhaps there is an untreated psychiatric condition, past trauma which has led to PTSD (which in turn developed into self-medicating behaviors), or perhaps communication skill building.

As providers, we need to challenge ourselves, society, and the CJ system as to how we approach managing offenders that become trapped within the system. If we are not going to commit to and fund treatment out in the community, then it is imperative that we provide these services within the walls of prison as one approach to avoid recidivism. Anything short of this seems to almost guarantee the revolving door that most prisons seem to have.

Credentialing helps protect the public. As ICB(Illinois Certification Board) (n.d.), formally known as the Illinois Alcohol & Other Drug Abuse Professional Certification Association, states in their Mission Statement that their goal is; "To protect the public by providing competency based credentialing of Human Service Professionals." ICB goes further explains, "ICB also encourages the highest ethical standards for all practitioners. ICB's professional standards meet or exceed all international standards for practitioners." Most clients will go into a treatment facility expecting to be treated by someone who is qualified and well trained. The client deserves this expectation, their family deserves it, the community deserves it, and we all deserve this expectation. However, does this always occur?

Title :77 of the IL Public Health Code, Chapter X Part 2060, is lovingly referred to as "Rule 2060". This is what guides and dictates how treatment is to be performed in the State of IL. Rest assured other states have their version of Rule 2060. In this Rule 2060, one would find very specific description of who can perform treatment of AODA services. This begins in Section 2060.309:

a) All professional staff providing clinical services as defined in this Part Shall:
   1. Hold certification as a CADC
   2. Be a licensed professional or licensed clinical professional counselor
   3. Be a physician licensed to practice medicine
   4. Be a licensed psychologist
   5. Be a licensed or licensed clinical social worker

There is no doubt that the above professionals are well trained. However, with the exception of the CADC, there is no mention or requirement, either stated or inferred, that these professionals are assumed to have had adequate training in AODA issues. It is hoped that the individual clinicians will take to heart their ethical obligation to only practice in areas in which they are sufficiently trained. However, there are administrators who will assume and in some cases demand that their clinicians perform tasks that is allowable per their license, not necessarily by the clinicians expertise.

Many disciplines train professionals to go into the frontline and work with clients. Yet as a profession and educational system, do we train these students adequately to face issues that are reported in as much as 50% of their practicum clients (Salyers, et al., 2006)? Most clinicians, once they have obtained their clinical hours and have passed their license to practice independently, are able to diagnose clients. It is understood that one can not obtain and maintain every certification and licensure that may be available in the State. However, given the enormity and complexity that AODA problems bring to the table, should an individual be able to diagnose someone with an AODA diagnosis without any formal training?

This paper only scratched the surface of how far and deep AODA issues run in the fabric of our society. We will continue to need qualified clinicians in many disciplines to help identify problems related to AODA and begin the intervention process. Formal training, coursework and seminars by accredited training programs appear to be one logical resolution to the above issue. AODA problems within our society will not be going away anytime soon. Therefore, this writer hopes that readers will agree that there is a need for additional qualified and knowledgeable clinicians, nurses, clergy, teachers and other disciplines to become more knowledgeable regarding AODA issues. This is truly a matter of life and death.

REFERENCES

Bennet, L.W. (2006). Substance abuse by men in partner abuse intervention programs: Current issues and promising trends. *Violence and Victims,* 23(2), Retrieved from: http://www.questia.com/library/1P3-1498060831/substance-abuse-by-men-in-partner-abuse-intervention

Brookhoff, D., O'Brin, K.K., Cook, C.S., Thompson, T.D., and Williams, C.C. (1997). Characteristics of participants in domestic violence. *Journal of the American Medical Association,* 277, 1369-1373. In G.L. Fisher and T.C. Harrison. (2009). *Substance abuse: Information for school counselors, social workers, therapists and counselors* (4ᵗʰ ed) Boston, MA: Allyn and Bacon.

Bureau of Justice Statistics. (1992). *Drugs, crime and the justice system* (NCJ 133652). Washington, D.C: U.S. Department of Justice. In L.A. Zilney. (2011). *Drugs: Policy, social costs, crime, and justice.* NJ: Prentice Hall.

Hall, M. N., Amodeo, M., Shaffer, H.J., & Vander Bilt, J. (2000). Social workers employed in substance abuse treatment agencies: A training needs assessment. *Social Work,* 45, 141-154. In M.J. Smith, J.W. Mickey, T. Whitaker, and T. Weismiller. (2006). Social workers in the substance abuse treatment field: A snapshot of service activities. *Health and Social Work,* 31(2) Retrieved from: http://www.questia.com/read/1G1-147057971/social-workers-in-the-substance-abuse-treatment-field

Illinois Certification Board. (n.d.). *Mission: To protect the public by providing competency based credentialing of Human Service Professionals.* Retrieved from: http://www.iaodapca.org/?page_id=167

Joint Committee on Administrative Rules; Administrative Code. Title 77: Public health chapter X: Department of human services subchapter d: Licensure part 2060; Alcoholism and substance abuse treatment and intervention licenses. (2003).

The National Center on Addiction and Substance Abuse (CASA) at Columbia University. (2010). *Behind bars II: Substance abuse and America's prison population.* Retrieved from: http://www.casacolumbia. org/templates/PressReleases.aspx?articleid=592&zoneid=79

Salyers, K.M., Ritchie, M.H., Cochrane, W.S., and Roseman, C.P. (2006). Inclusion of substance abuse training in CACREP- accredited programs. *Journal of Addiction and Offender Counseling, 27(1), 1–22.* Retrieved from*: http://www.questia.com/read/1G1-153691521/ inclusion-of-substance-abuse-training-in-cacrep-accredited*

Substance Abuse and Mental Health Services Administration. (2011). *Drug abuse warning network, 2009: National estimates of drug-related emergency room department visits.* Retrieved from: http://www. samhsa.gov/data/2k13/DAWN127/sr127-DAWN-highlights.htm

Substance Abuse and Mental Health Services Administration. (2009). *Substance abuse treatment: Addressing the specific needs of women: A Treatment Improvement Protocol TIP 51.* HHS Publication No. (SMA) 09-4426 Retrieved from: http://www.samhsa.gov/shin

BINGE DRINKING ON COLLEGE CAMPUS
by Kimberly Groll LCPC, CADC< CAMT

Underage drinking is a concern no matter if the individual is at home or going off to college. Dealing with a DUI for underage drinking and driving is a bigger concern. I have seen the affects of young adolescents who have been charged with underage drinking and getting their first DUI. When I hear their stories and how sorry they are for making a bad decision for one night of drinking with getting behind the wheel of an automobile, it truly is heartbreaking knowing their lives have changed forever.

First of all they are inexperienced drivers with only a few years of driving on the road. Add alcohol to the inexperience and now their overall perception is compromised.

Adolescents don't have the reasoning skills in place and don't always make good decisions. They believe they will never get caught or it will never happen to them. Too often it does happen and they are left with the consequences that follow.

I know of individuals who were accepted to the college of their choice. After getting a DUI this changed their plans to attend that college because they feared they would not be able to drink the way they attended when they entered their first year on campus. There are a few things wrong with this type of thinking. First of all, it appears the drinking is a priority, and secondly their choice of college is now compromised with making plans to attend a community college. Don't get me wrong; there is nothing wrong with attending a community college. What I find troublesome is not following through with their original plans with attending the college of their choice due to worrying about fitting into the drinking crowd and not being able to drink as they planned due to getting a DUI.

What are the chances of a person you know drinking too much when they go off to college? When a person leaves home for the first time and experiences life on their own, we hope they use their better judgment and make good choices. Many do; however, many will experiment and will want to fit in with going along with the rest of the crowd.

When parents bring their adolescents in to see me prior to leaving for college with concerns of drinking and smoking marijuana in which they know has taken place, they want to know what to do. They are concerned about their child leaving for college with continuing to use alcohol and drugs and getting into trouble. These are good kids, making good grades, and when I meet them they state their use is minimal. They all have good intentions on keeping their grades up, and they claim to not overdo it with drinking or smoking marijuana. As a counselor I need to bring awareness to their using patterns and to make them aware of when they are minimizing, rationalizing or justifying their behaviors.

Counselor Tip: If a person is **minimizing** their use, he or she would play down the amount they are drinking or using drugs.

If a person is **rationalizing** their behavior he or she would be convincing themselves it was okay to drink or use drugs because they are doing well in school and keeping up with their grades.

If a person is **justifying** their behavior he or she would accept their pattern of drinking or using drugs because that is what all their friends are doing and they want to fit in and be like everyone else.

It is important for the individual to understand when he or she is using these patterns of thinking. I inform my clients about these three cognitive distortions and to be aware if they are indeed using any of the patterns of thinking when drinking or using drugs.

If a student has entered into their college years and starts to fall behind with his/her assignments, this could be the first signs of alarm. I know students have good intentions to study and to write papers that are needed to fulfill their obligations; however, if a night of drinking interferes with their original plans, and they put their studies off, they need to take a deeper look at themselves and realize this can be the beginning stages of losing control.

Dear Counselor column written on Binge Drinking on College Campus

With many adolescents graduating from high school and planning to attend college, awareness about binge drinking on college campuses needs to be addressed. Many adolescents will be leaving their home for the first time and many of them will have and feel a new sense of freedom. They will be away from the everyday rules and regulations set forth by their parents. They will need to learn to balance their time, manage their studies, and of course they will be meeting new friends while experiencing the college lifestyle. For some this means buckling down and applying themselves. For others this means time to party without being told what to do and how to do it.

As an addictions counselor for drugs and alcohol, I have counseled many adolescents who started partying in high school and carry this with them into their college years. What concerns me as a counselor is the amount of drinking that occurs on a college campus. I hear stories of all sorts; I also am called when the reality of drinking or drug use turns into trouble.

Some of the things I've heard are, "I can't wait until I get into college, then I am going to do what I want to do." "I will be able to smoke my dope or drink anytime I want without my parent's drug testing me." "I thought I would be able to keep up with my studies after a night of partying; however, I just kept getting further and further behind in my classes."

This is scary to hear as a counselor/parent, and I have to wonder how many parents would be willing to pay for their children's education if they knew their child's first interest in going off to college is partying and secondly trying to keep up with his or her studies.

A parent wrote to me this month with this same concern and I thought it would be important to bring information about college binge drinking to this month's column.

Dear Counselor,

My son will be returning to college this year. I am really concerned because his first year was not that productive. He barely passed his courses and had to go to summer school in order to make up for some credits he lost due to his choices of drinking and having a good time. He has openly admitted to us the amount of partying that goes on at the campus. I am not proud of this as a parent and yet I don't know what to do about the situation. Do you think I have to worry about the amount of drinking he is doing, especially underage? Or, is this something he will grow out of?

C. W. (Naperville) Dear C. W.

I would be concerned in how much your son is drinking, especially since he is underage. I would want to know his pattern of drinking and how much he is drinking during the week or on weekends. At what age did he first start to drink? Does he go on binges? Has he experienced blackouts?

When a person starts to drink at an early age he builds a tolerance. He will need to drink more in able to reach the same affects he is seeking. The earlier he starts the more dangerous this can become for an individual.

It would be important to discuss how alcohol abuse affects him and the family. You may want to sit down with him prior to leaving for college and have a family meeting. You may want to discuss your concerns for his safety and educate him about the seriousness of alcohol and the possible trouble that can follow him for the rest of his life if he is caught doing something under the influence of alcohol. If he is open to speaking with you, perhaps you may be able to identify his needs and issues.

I see so many cases after the damage has been done. If you recognize any unusual behavior, it is important to address the issues right away. Sending your child off to college, or just off for the day with knowing things are not right with your child, would be sweeping the problem under the carpet.

Having a child see a counselor can sometimes help to regain balance. You may feel better knowing your child is addressing his issues rather than taking a chance with him getting into trouble later on with having a possible record which would follow him for the rest of his life. He could also put himself in a position to hurt himself or someone else under the influence and these are situations you will not be able to change.

Sincerely, Counselor Kimberly

I would also like to address the secondhand victims of college binge drinking:

44% of college students binge drink at least once every two weeks. Binge drinking equals 5 or more drinks in a row for a male; 4 or more drinks in a row for a female.

87% of college students have suffered from "Secondary Binge Effects" caused by other's drinking.

68% had studying/sleeping interrupted

54% had to take care of a drunken student

34% been insulted or humiliated

26% experienced unwanted sexual advances

20% had a serious argument or quarrel

15% had property damaged
13% have been pushed, hit, or assaulted
2% have been a victim of sexual assault or date rape

College drinking not only affects the person drinking but it also affects the ones who choose not to drink. It is important to realize the seriousness of underage drinking and the effects it has on everyone.

College kids do have a choice to request alcohol free dorms to avoid these problems.

A Multimodal Approach to Relapse Prevention

By Robert F. Bollendorf Ed.D. CADC and Frank Salvatini M.Ed.,CSADC, NCACll,MISAll.

Counseling and therapy is all about helping change human processes. Let's start with a simple example. What a person weighs is a number on a scale, but to change that number any person has to focus on a process. One of those processes is eating, and most people go about changing the number on the scale by changing their diet. Some counselors might also get the person to increase their exercise. That is good because now we have two processes involved in change and even if the person is successful in just one the number on the scale may change.

But a really good counselor may also nibble (couldn't resist the pun) around other human processes as well. What about how the person thinks about food? Do they use food to reward themselves, or to sooth certain emotions? Are their certain memories around food? Was a certain birthday party a highlight of growing up, and does eating recreate that felling for the person. What is their relationship with food?

Sally began to see food as her enemy. Others may see it as their best friend.

Another import point for counselors to keep in mind is that any process is always ongoing. Whether the person we are working with has a problem with food or drugs they are never finished. Some people may still remember the famous Nike slogan of "Just Do It", but our favorite and one more fitting for our purposes here came from another commercial perhaps some of you will remember. It started with a man running down a city street with tall buildings in the background. Occasionally on those building you would see flashes of sports stars doing what they do best. But the important part for us came right at the end when simply written on the screen were the words:

"There is no finish line."

In sports there are two important times for any athlete. One is the event. Whether it is a race, a game, or a match an event has a beginning middle and an end. Once that event is over nothing can change it, but training, however, is different. There, like the end of our commercial, there

208

is no finish line. It is never over and also importantly it is always changing. Like life itself, there are good days and bad days, and many that seem the same. But a process never really stays the same. To introduce this from an addictions concept we are either recovering or relapsing. All of us are recovering in some ways and relapsing in others.

A striking example of this changing process is children who have been victims of war, draught, and famine and gone a period of time without eating. Those children have to be taught how to eat again. Part of that is physiological. A muscle that is not used atrophies. A friend of ours recently had a serious heart attack and was bedridden for several weeks and also had a tracheotomy. Though he is now walking, he still can't swallow or stand on his own.

There are two ways in which we relapse in any process. One of those ways is to not to use a process.

Atrophy of a process occurs if there is little or no appropriate utilization of that process. An example of a process that can deteriorate in this way is communication. Take a young couple in love—engaged to marry. It would not be uncommon for that couple to spend a lot of time communicating with each other. They go out on a date and they talk. Then the next day they call each other on the phone and they talk about what they talked about the night before. They might say: "I'm not sure what you meant by this and I was sort of hurt by that." They process most of their communication and then they get married.

After some time, they may begin to think: "Gee now we're living together and we spend all this time together so we really don't have to communicate anymore. Besides, we spent all that time while we were dating getting to know each other and now we know each other, so why talk about it." Now, as that couple begins to talk and communicate less often, their ability to connect with each other deteriorates. Misunderstandings and resentments increase and the couple no longer talks about these issues.

The second way in which a process can deteriorate (or relapse occurs) is if it is practiced inappropriately, or done "the wrong way." To clarify this, let's again use an example from physiology. Let's look at the heart. When you subject the heart to exercise, it also beats faster. But for some reason or other, when it beats faster under stressful conditions it not only doesn't grow stronger, it grows weaker—as opposed to exercise which makes the heart grow stronger.

The same inappropriate use can occur with communication. Our married couple can further spiral downward if they communicate in ways designed to win rather than to resolve an issue between them.

They may begin using tactics like name calling, blaming, screaming and yelling.

On the other hand there is only one way in which a process can improve and that is to practice healthy uses of the process regularly. We believe there are six major reasons for utilizing these concepts in counseling.

The first is it is a holistic approach.

Second it identifies a number of processes in recovery and relapse.

Third it gives the client several choices on what to work on in daily life to continue to move him toward a stronger recovery program.

Fourth it helps them to identify that may lead toward using their drug of choice again.

As Gorski points our relapse is a process that ends in the returning to an addiction. Many addicts think using again is the start of a relapse when actually there are many signs of relapse long before that point. This is analogous to a heart patient thinking they are fine as long as they don't have another heart attack.

A fifth reason is it helps the counselor to assess relapse and recovery issues.

And finally it clearly delineates the roles of the counselor and client responsibilities.

The counselor's roles are:

1. To help the client focus on process rather than results
2. To help the client identify issues of recovery and relapse
3. To teach new processes that lead to a stronger recovery such as mindfulness meditation, cognitive restructuring, and anger management
4. To listen and respond (perhaps with motivational interviewing techniques) as the client works through their priorities
5. To help the client to identify and overcome obstacles to recovery

The responsibility of the client is to practice the new process that he and his counselor have agreed to on a regular basis in between sessions. If the client does not practice what they are learning then counseling will probably be only minimally helpful no matter how long he stays in counseling.

There are two potential misinterpretations of this approach. The first is that the client should be addressing all of these at once. That would be a mistake. Our goal would be for a client to be working on one or two items at a time until a level of mastery is attained and then moving to another. The client can either be working on eliminating a relapse process or improving a recovery process.

The second misinterpretation is that a counselor or client should not panic if a number of relapse processes are identified. As stated earlier we are all in both processes at the same time. The goal is to increase the recovery side while decreasing the relapse side.

Some years ago Arnold Lazarus utilized an acronym BASIC ID to identify the human processes he worked with in Multimodal Behavior Therapy. We utilize the Basic Id with modifications to fit into a holistic model of relapse prevention.

The "B" in BASIC ID stands for behaviors. We have listed several behaviors at the end of this paper. So at this point, we will just mention an example in each category for point of clarification. For instance, an example of a behavior which tends to add to an alcoholics recovery would be regular attendance and participation at AA meetings. An example of a relapsing behavior might be when participation at meetings begins to decline or when the nature of that participation becomes self-pitying, complaining and inappropriate—such as someone reminiscing about "the good old days."

The "A" in BASIC ID stands for affect or feeling. Recovery in this area usually starts with just being able to identify feelings. Am I happy, sad, mad or glad? Relapsing feelings have been identified by Gorski and others as anger, false pride, self pity, etc.

The "S" in BASIC ID, according to Lazarus stands for somatic concerns. These may be complaints such as headaches, stiffness and insomnia on the relapsing side. Recovery may be learning relaxation or mindfulness techniques. For purposes of addiction, we have added two additional categories. These are spirituality and sexuality. Spirituality is considered by many to be an important part of recovery. We define spirituality as moving toward a set of values. For instance, the recovering person who was an environmentalist and worked towards improving the environment would be recovering spiritually. The person who is acting in ways outside the values he has established is relapsing in that way. The person who values honesty is relapsing when he lies.

In Sexuality, the beginning takes place with answering the question "who am I as a man or woman?" Relapsing could be seen as viewing sex only as something to be performed or as a way of controlling another individual.

The first "I" in BASIC ID has two meanings. One is self-image--meaning the ways the recovering person sees or feels about him or herself. It is quite evident here that the recovering person would have a declining self-image.

The second "I" is memory. The goal for memory may be to find a healthy balance between focusing on the present and the past—using the past only to help us avoid the same problems in the present.

The "C" in BASIC ID quite simply refers to cognitive messages. These are intricately tied to feelings (affect) in that feelings are caused by beliefs or cognitive messages individuals send themselves. Examples of healthy cognitive messages would be "I've done my best for today." Or "easy does it" and so on. Relapsing is indicated when cognitive messages are unrealistic or self-deprecating. For example, "I'm too dumb to go back to school" or "I've got to finish all 12 steps of AA this week.

The second "I" in BASIC ID stands for two things. They are interpersonal communication and intellectual pursuits. Examples of interpersonal communication have been presented earlier in this presentation. In terms of intellectual pursuits, recovery would be an endeavor resulting in self-enhancing knowledge, such as enrolling in a college course about a particular area of interest. Relapse would be the absence or decline of such pursuits such as spending a large amount of leisure time watching TV reruns.

The "D" in BASIC ID covers four types of processes. They are: diet, drugs, decision-making and defense mechanisms. Examples of healthy eating habits might be to eat several small meals each day, eating high complex carbohydrates and moderate protein meals. Relapse potential can be seen in skipping meals or eating nutritionally deficient foods such as refined sugar, white flour, etc.

Relapsing with drugs is almost self-explanatory. It might be switching the addiction to another mood-altering substance or using a drug for purposes not intended for that drug, etc. Recovery should include only appropriately prescribed drugs and limited use of any mood-altering drugs (for dual-diagnosis patients.) That would also include appropriate use of necessary over-the-counter medications such as aspirin, vitamin supplements, etc.

Decision-making is often difficult for the recovering client especially early in recovery. Decisions should be made promptly, but should be carefully thought out using the data available.

Again, defense mechanisms are self-evident. Relapse takes place when one denies or rationalizes reality. Recovery is taking place when one looks honestly and openly at him or herself and the environment.

B

-
- Talking at meetings
- Regular attendance at meetings
- Realistic daily plan
- Goals: short, medium, long-term
- Exercise

- Sober fun
- Initiating friendships
- Beginning new behaviors
- Meets problems head on
- Using realistic problem approaches
- Becoming interdependent
- Taking care of self

A

- Peace, love, serenity
- Recognizing and expressing feelings in the moment and to the degree which is equal to the external situation
- Love of self
- Security in self
- Faces & expresses own acceptance of both positive and negative feelings

Behavior

- Stops sharing at meetings
- Stops going to meetings
- Loss of daily structure
- Failure to plan

- Attending parties where alcohol and drugs are present
- Going to bars
- Increase in isolation
- Busy doing things for others
- Becomes rigid and repetitive
- Over commitment

- Weak boundaries
- Neglecting self

Affect

- Anxiety
- Rarely shows outward one's emotions
- Feelings jumbled - can't tell one from another
- Easily angered, resentful
- Loneliness, fear
- Insecurity, guilt - as when something given to them.
- Feels harassed, pressured, angry, victimized, unappreciated, used, bored, empty, worthless.
- Depression, listlessness
- Immature wish to "be happy"

S

- Regular use of relaxation and mindfulness techniques
- Person aware of body and relaxation
- Regular self-care routine
- Developing appreciation for each of the five senses

- Sexuality as a natural function
- Sex is not something to be performed, but lived
- Sex is communicating love & feelings for another - part of a committed relationship
- Sex is communication of love, wants, and needs
- Sex is communication of who you are - at an intimate level

- Daily meditation following a program
- Having a spiritual advisor
- Regular spiritual reading
- Gratitude comes after assessing life
- Renewal, acceptance of self
- Decrease in materialism

Sensation

- Experiences many vague aches & pains
- Headaches, colitis, increased stress, physical problems
- Little attention to self-care
- Afraid of pleasures

Sexuality

- Sexuality as performance oriented
- Promiscuity
- Obsessive thinking

- Following a set of values decreases

- Sex use for control, not communication
- Loss of interest in sex

Spirituality

- Return of narcissism
- Begins acting in more selfish ways
- Higher Power seems distant without connectedness
-
- Having a lot of "shoulds"
- Increase i n materialism

I

- Improving self-image

- Self-acceptance
- Self forgiveness

- Balance of living in the here and now with enough looking back in order to realistically appraise and avoid problems related to drinking
- Uses past to assess current problems
- Uses past to avoid repeating mistakes

C

- Positive self-talk
- Improved concentration
- Realistic_ perception of drinking and drug use
- Rational thinking

- Realistic expectations and evaluations

Self-Image

- Declining self-image
- Lack of confidence in ability to stay sober
- Blame self for everything
- Reject praise
- Believe that others could not possibly love them

Imagery – Memories

- Glorifying memories of drinking or using phase
- Ignoring the past or obsessing about the past
- Focus on instances of sexual, physical, and emotional abuse, neglect, abandonment, alcoholism and addictions.

Cognitive Messages

- Negative self-talk
- Diminished ability to concentrate
- Thoughts of social drinking
- Assumption, awfulizing
- Catastrophasizing
- Perfectionist, tunnel vision
- Assumption of inappropriate responsibility

I

- Feeling talk
- Non judgmental

- Assertiveness
- Improved listening skills
- Non defensive
- Trusting
- Honest
- Open
- Accepting
- Helpful
- Acceptance of help from others

D

- Regular eating
- Balanced meals
- Low fat, salt, and sugar
- Emphasis on nutrition

- Use of prescribed non-mood altering drugs as indicated by professional
- Appropriate use of non-prescription drugs (aspirin, etc.)

Interpersonal Communication

- Blaming
- Controlling
- Passive/aggressive
- Distracting
- Defensive
- Rigid controlling through:
- helplessness, guilt coercion threats, advice giving domination
- begging and bribes
- lying
- No - or weak – boundaries
- Placating others

Diet

- Irregular eating habits
- Junk food
- Increased fat, salt, and sugar
- Emotional substitution of foods

Drugs

- Increase use of caffeine, nicotine, and other over-the-counter drugs
- Controlled drinking and/or out-of-control drinking
- Use of drugs for mood-altering effects.

- Making timely realistic decisions based on the information available.

- Honest and open view of self, others, and environment

Decision making

- Procrastination or impulsiveness in decisions
- Worry, stress, fretting

Denial

- Rationalization
- Projection
- Minimizing
- Denial

STUDY QUESTION

IN THE PAPER "A MULTIMODAL Approach to Relapse Prevention" there are several examples in the BASIC ID of recovery and relapse. What are five examples from the Brandt family of recovery and five examples of relapse?

BIBLIOGRAPHY

Bean, Margaret, "Clinical Implications of Models .for Recovery from Alcoholism", *The Addictive Behaviors,* Shaffer, Howard and Barry, Stimmel (eds). The Haworth Press, Inc., 1984. Pp. 91-104.

Gorski, Terrence T. and Miller, Merlene. <u>Staying Sober, A Guide to Relapse Prevention.</u> Independence, Missouri, Herald House Publishers, 1986.

Gorski, Terrence T. and Miller, Merlene. <u>Counseling For Relapse Prevention.</u> Hazel Crest, Illinois, Human Ecology Systems, Inc., 1979.

Lazarus, Arnold A. The <u>Practice of Multimodal Therapy: Systematic, Comprehensive, and Effective Psychotherapy.</u> New York: McGraw-Hill, 1981.

McCrady, Barbara S., PhD., Smith, Delia E., "Implications of Cognitive Impairment for the Treatment of Alcoholism," *Alcoholism: Clinical and Experimental Research,* Vol. 10 No. 2, March/April 1986.

Wiseman, J. P., "Sober Comportment: Patterns and Perspectives of Alcohol Addiction," *Journal of Studies on Alcohol,* 1981 42(1), 106-126.

Miller, W. R., Rollnick, S., "Motivational Interviewing: Preparing People for Change." Guilford Press 2002.

Printed in the United States
By Bookmasters